Knight of the Road

San Quentin Prison photograph of Ham White, as Henry Miller, taken in 1891. Courtesy: California State Archives, Sacramento, California.

Knight
of the Road

*The Life of Highwayman
Ham White*

By Mark Dugan

Swallow Press/Ohio University Press
Athens

Swallow Press/Ohio University Press books are printed on acid-free paper ∞

Library of Congress Cataloging-in-Publication Data

Dugan, Mark, 1941-
    Knight of the road : the life of highwayman
Ham White / by Mark Dugan.
        p.   cm.
    Includes bibliographical references and index.
    ISBN 0-8040-0936-8. — ISBN 0-8040-0940-6
(pbk.)
    1. White, Ham, 1854-1900. 2. Outlaws—South-
west, New—Biography. 3. Coaching—Southwest,
New—History—19th century. 4. Southwest,
New—History—1848- I. Title.
F786.W578D84 1990
979'.02'092—dc20
[B]   90-39441
                                                        CIP

To Donaly
WHO WENT THE EXTRA MILE

Contents

Contents

Illustrations

Acknowledgments

The research material cited in this book was, at times, extremely difficult to uncover. Fortunately, I had help and would like to express my sincere appreciation to the following individuals whose efforts contributed to the entire contents of this book.

I could never have started this book without the unselfish contributions of my good friend, Mr. Donaly Brice of the Texas State Archives. How many hours of his own time he devoted to this research I do not know. He never would tell me. What I do know is that every single time I needed help, he provided it. Except for the Federal Court records, Donaly one way or another helped me obtain every bit of the Texas research information. This book belongs to Donaly Brice as much as it does to me.

I offer my gratitude to everyone who added the necessary information to complete this book, and list them state by state.

ARIZONA: Marianna Hansin, Betsy Howard, Edwin C. Rogers, Department of Library, Archives, and Public Records, Phoenix; Lisa Henry, Office of the Clerk of the Superior Court of Pinal County, Florence; Dr. C.L. Sonnichsen, Tucson.

CALIFORNIA: Joseph P. Samora, Archivist, California State Archives, Sacramento; Irene Mahan, Sacramento; Susan Dewberry, Federal Archives and Record Center, Laguna Niguel; Elaine M. Gilleran, Wells Fargo Bank History Museum, San Francisco.

COLORADO: Sharon Elfenbein, Denver; Catherine Engel, Colorado Historical Society, Denver; Joel Barker and Dan Nealand, Federal Archives and Record Center, Denver.

DISTRICT OF COLUMBIA: R. Michael McReynolds, Assistant Chief of the Judicial, Fiscal and Social Branch, National Archives and Record Center, Washington; Marie Melchiori, Vienna, Virginia.

NEW YORK: Coreen P. Hallenbeck, Albany; Anthony Frantozzi, Federal Archives and Record Center, Bayonne, New Jersey.

TEXAS: Ed Bartholomew, Fort Davis; Barbara Rust, Federal Archives and Record Center, Fort Worth; Laura G. Cunningham, Austin; Viola White Gentry, Austin; Beulah White Davis, Austin; Dorothy Cavitt, Austin; Kate Cordts, San Antonio City Library, San Antonio; Retired Judge Moore Johanson, Llano; Mary Schrader White, Bexar County District Court, San Antonio; Gayle Metcalf and Shelly Schaper, Texas Department of Corrections, Huntsville; Dr. Robert Pierce, Director of the Texas Prison Archives, Huntsville; Ken Johnson, Huntsville; Susan Perry, *The San Angelo Standard-Times* Office, San Angelo; Polly Crawford, Angelo State University Library, San Angelo; Mack Mullins, Waco; Dr. C. Richard King, Stephenville; Shirley Wilhelm, Bastrop County Clerk, Bastrop; Reverend Kenneth Kesselus, Calvary Episcopal Church, Bastrop.

WEST VIRGINIA: Carol Warner, Archives and History Division, Department of Culture and History, Charleston.

NORTH CAROLINA: Bobby Y. Emory, Raleigh; Pam Toms, North Carolina Department of Archives and History, Raleigh; Ray Steckenrider, Raleigh; Polly Culler, Raleigh; Peter Jones and Elaine Jones, Fairview; Bill White, Photographer, Raleigh.

Special thanks for the help I received from my friends and fellow authors John Boessenecker of San Francisco and Chuck Parsons of Wisconsin. This book became a reality because of the invaluable editorial suggestions of Francis L. Fugate of El Paso, Texas and the faith of my Editor, Holly Panich.

I can never repay my wife Sarah for the many hours of work that she contributed in completing this book. I could never have finished it alone.

Preface

This is a storybook. Although every incident and event that occurs in the contents is absolutely true and supported by documentation, it is still a storybook. If I had submitted this book as fiction to a publisher of Western novels, I fully believe it would have been rejected on the grounds that it was too unbelievable. But as the old adage goes, truth is stranger than fiction.

I first became interested in Ham White when I was writing *The Grey Fox: The True Story Of Bill Miner, Last of the Old Time Bandits*. In researching old newspapers, several times I ran across the exploits of one Henry Burton, the alias White used in Colorado. While researching the Miner book, I discovered that Miner was just one in a series of stage robbers that repeatedly victimized the Barlow-Sanderson stagecoach line in southern Colorado in a short eight-month period. This also resulted in a third book titled, *Bandit Years: A Gathering of Wolves*, a history concerning these robberies, which included White's exploits.

Uncovering his early history in Texas and, of course, his Colorado escapades, I then lost track of White after he committed two more stage robberies in Texas following his release from prison in 1887. For a year and a half I searched in frustration but could find no trace of him.

During my initial research, I contacted Donaly Brice at the Texas State Archives in Austin for help. After the year and a half unfruitful search for White's latter history, I received a phone call from Mrs. Laura G. Cunningham from Austin, Texas. Mrs. Cunningham is a great-niece of Ham White and had contacted me through Donaly. She requested permission to obtain a copy of the material I had written for *Bandit Years: A Gathering of Wolves* regarding Ham White. I gave her the material and she, in turn, promised to send me any information she could obtain. In two months Mrs. Cunningham sent me a copy of a letter written in 1941 to a relative by the warden of the Texas State Penitentiary regarding White.

This letter opened all doors and I found the reason I could not trace him: He had lived for twelve years under another alias. In short, I was able to obtain all pertinent documentated research to finish White's biography.

As his story unfolded, I was utterly amazed at his extraordinary career. I have had immense pleasure in researching and writing his life history.

After completing White's biography, I think it fortunate that I only lost track of him for only eighteen months, for many others before me lost him for much longer periods of time than that.

Mark Dugan, 1987

Introduction

Let us Give the Devil His Due

Ham White was born in the wrong century. He should have been a bold and gallant English highwayman in the seventeenth- and eighteenth-century days of Claude Duval and Dick Turpin. Instead, born in Bastrop County, Texas in the hectic decade preceding the Civil War, he grew up to be the premier stagecoach robber in the United States.

Some may question this statement and refer to the exploits of Charles E. Boles alias Black Bart, the notorious California stage robber of the 1880s. It is true that the noted highwayman waylaid more stages than White, four to be exact, but after he was caught, convicted, and served his prison term, Black Bart never robbed another stage.[1] On the other hand, White, after serving three of his prison sentences, could not wait to get out and hold up another stage. Both bandits, however, did have one thing in common, they always robbed stagecoaches alone. In White's case, this was due to a marked distrust of others and his antisocial nature. Texas ranger N.A. Jennings, a member of Lee Hall's Company of rangers which captured White in 1877, made this statement comparing the two bandits: "He [White] has been confounded many times with the notorious Black Bart, but was far more daring than that 'knight of the road.' "[2]

Allowing this to be fact, it raises the question why Ham White never received the recognition and popular notoriety of a Black Bart, William Quantrill, Jesse James, or a Billy the Kid? His name and career escaped the attention of the dime novelists, pulp writers, and hacks of his day because Ham White was not always known as Ham White. Reverting to several aliases during his career, he remained in anonymity, except for several obscure pages in a few books.[3] However, fictional stories based on White's escapades have been written.

Andy Adams' tale, "He Had Collided with Lead in Texas," gives the reader a very enjoyable, amusing, yet accurate account of White's 1881 Colorado stage robbery. The protagonist called Baugh, a passenger on the victimized stage, was in reality Theodore Baughman, a personal friend of Adams. Evidently Adams based his story on the Colorado newspaper accounts of the robbery as Theodore Baughman was not an actual stage passenger during the holdup.[4]

Another story, supposedly woven around the habits and manners of Ham White, was written by O. Henry and titled "The Hiding of Black Bill." During his imprisonment in the Ohio Penitentiary, William Sydney Porter wrote this story and many others under the pen name of O. Henry. Henry's character, named Ham, was a train robber known only as "Black Bill," and tells his story of hiding out at a sheep ranch in the Nueces country under the alias of Percival St. Clair after robbing a train. In the article, "Background and Patterns of O. Henry's Texas Badman Stories," J.S. Gallegly offers the reader a comparative analysis between O. Henry's Ham and Ham White. After reading O. Henry's story, the only similarity between the two men, as far as this author can ascertain, is that both are named "Ham." The description, actions, and habits of O. Henry's Ham bears no resemblance to the real Ham White.[5]

White's authentic life history makes it apparent that in his complex mind he considered life a game in which everyone must play by his rules. Sometimes these rules caused him to think and act senselessly and illogically; at other times he devised plans that bordered on brilliance. According to his standards it was permissible to rob and plunder and, in turn, to be captured and punished. It was also permissible to escape punishment in any way possible and then start the cycle again. What was not acceptable was for those who arrested and prosecuted him to trick, harass, or threaten him. When this happened, White became enraged and fought back. During these times he could be dangerous, though basically he was non-violent. Records show that during his twenty-five year career he was convicted and imprisoned in various penal institutions six times; made eight escape attempts, of which five were successful; legally finagled his way out of three penitentiaries; and attacked twenty-four stagecoaches.

White also developed his own code of honor. During his stage robberies he was always courteous and considerate to his victims, more than often conversing with them or putting them at ease with his jocular commentary. He was gentlemanly and chivalrous, refusing to rob or molest women, the handicapped, the elderly, or the laboring man. His stage robberies were classic and he holds the dubious distinction of single-handedly holding up two stagecoaches simultaneously.

White could have been called not only a knight of the road, but also a king of the flim-flam artists. With seemingly honest conviction, he worked his duplicity, cunning, and deception on several federal and state law officers as well as the leading criminal law firm in the Southwest; the leading newspaper in Bastrop County, Texas; a United States attorney; a United States Congressman; two Federal Judges; the personnel of two penitentiaries including the wardens; two governors; the Attorney General of the United States; almost the entire population of Bastrop County, Texas; a general manager of an entire railroad line; the United States judicial system; and a President of the United States. An unbelievable record but nonetheless true.

White left no personal recollections or autobiography to gain a better understanding of his character. The only recourse is to accept the words of those who knew him well. Ironically, those who did know him were not his friends or companions, they were his adversaries; Sheriffs, United States Marshals, and Post Office Inspectors. U.S. Deputy Postal Inspector L. Cass Carpenter gave the most perceptive analysis. Carpenter, assigned to the Denver, Colorado office, became well acquainted with White, his history and his escapades in Colorado. In his statement, Carpenter refers to White as Burton, the alias White used in Colorado. The following is his accurate and farsighted summation of Ham White:

> I regard Burton as the most daring, skillful, accomplished highwayman of whom history gives an account. He is neither brutal or uneducated, but rather the reverse. If there can be anything manly in robbing a stagecoach, probably Burton manifested that trait. . . . Burton says he never yet robbed a woman or a cripple, nor a poor man if he knew it.[6]

Almost as important as Carpenter's evaluation of White was the view of the press. Of numerous articles written about him throughout his career this commentary from *The Daily Democratic Statesman* in Austin, Texas seems to be the most illuminating.

> Ham White, with all his faults, has good points. He is chivalrous and brave, and generous to the poor. When robbing stagecoach passengers he would hand back the scrapings of a poor man's pocket, saying "I

won't take that, you look like you had to work hard for your money," and when the well-dressed and more flush passengers would ask to retain enough money to pay a night's hotel bill, he would never refuse; this being evident that he, perhaps, has himself felt the pangs of hunger and fully appreciated the merits of a "square meal" to a traveler. Say what men may of the deviltries and wickedness and death-deserving crimes of White, he was not without virtues to ennoble his blackened frame. Very certainly he is the bravest of the brave. . . . Let us give the devil his due, and if White be a product of Texas whiskey and of Texas vices, let us not forget to give due justice to the man who was the product of the vices and virtues of Texas.[7]

Throughout his lifetime Ham White remained true to his strange code of honor and, as Carpenter brought out, even won the grudging respect of many officers of the law. Regardless of his sordid career, one cannot help developing a certain fondness for the bandit, perhaps actually "pulling" for him at times, especially during his pathetic, later years when the heyday of his stage robbing career was over. He was America's answer to Robin Hood, a true Knight of the Road.

PART I

A Product of Texas Vices and Virtues

CHAPTER ONE

Nothing Short of
"An Eye for an Eye and a Tooth for a Tooth"
Would Satisfy Me

Early March is often a harbinger of spring in central Texas and it was likely a day such as this in 1877 when a weatherworn and saddle-weary young man of just over medium height chanced upon a stopped stagecoach between Gatesville and Waco.

At first his large, round blue-grey eyes showed no more than a passing interest but on noticing the affluence of some of the passengers, they opened wider as a trace of a smile spread across his broad mouth. Likely no one in the stage gave the man any more than a passing glance, being used to seeing down-on-their-luck and broke, wandering cowboys. If the passengers had noticed him they would have been right about him being broke, but they would never guess by his plain but pleasant countenance that he was wanted for murder and cattle theft or what he was at that moment contemplating.

Leaning back in his saddle the man turned his horse, rode to the nearest house and politely asked in a soft, refined voice when the next stage would arrive. Receiving the information he gave his thanks and rode to a nearby hill. Finding a secluded spot screened by brush, he waited throughout the long night for the morning stage.

On hearing the lumbering sound of the stage from Waco to Gatesville the man quickly pulled up a crude mask made from his bandana. Remaining in his saddle to hide a stiff right leg, he wheeled his horse, leveled his revolver at the stage driver and ordered him to stop. Thus began the long stage robbing career of Hamilton White III, better known as Ham, who was destined to become the premier stagecoach robber in United States history.

Ham White descended from a long line of respected and affluent ancestors. His great-grandfather, Jeremiah White (circa 1740–1788) was born in Dinwiddie County, Virginia and moved to the eastern portion of Pittsylvania County, Virginia in 1778. Ham's grandfather, Hamilton White I (circa 1770–1832), remained in Pittsylvania County; his son, Hamilton White II was born in about 1808. Hamilton II married Tabitha Hutchings (born circa 1815), on November 5, 1833; their daughter, Melissa, was born September 26, 1834 while the family still lived in Pittsylvania County.[1]

By 1835 Hamilton II had decided to emigrate. In January, 1836 he arrived in Bastrop County, Texas and staked a claim on Mayhaw Creek in the Cedar Creek community, about ten miles west of Bastrop and around twenty miles southeast of Austin. The Whites picked a very inopportune time to settle in Texas as the Anglo-Texans had begun their revolution against Mexican rule the previous November. When news reached Bastrop that the Alamo had fallen on March 6, a general panic spread and families hurriedly packed what they could and fled eastward for safety.

Since most of the men were serving with the army, a company of rangers aided the women and children in their flight. Although Hamilton Whites's name does not appear as serving with the army, it was likely he had enlisted in Bastrop's "Mina Volunteers." The rangers remained at Bastrop until Mexican General Gaona and around 700 troops arrived on April 1. The Mexican troops entered the deserted village and after plundering it, departed for San Felipe. Following the departure of the Mexicans, the Indians destroyed what was left of Bastrop. After the defeat of Santa Anna's Mexican Army at San Jacinto on April 21, the refugee families returned to Bastrop and begun rebuilding the homes they had lost.

From late 1837 until April, 1839 the towns of Bastrop and Waterloo (now Austin) vied for the capitalship of the Republic of Texas. On April 25, 1838, in a report to the Second Congress, Bastrop citizens pledged over ten thousand acres of privately owned land on condition that the capital be located in Bastrop. One of the signers was Hamilton White II who offered three hundred acres of land located within twelve miles of Bastrop. It was a vain effort for on April 13, 1839 Waterloo was chosen as the capital site.

During Bastrop County's early years no one was exempt from the danger of Indian raids. During the later 1830s Hamilton II had contracted to supply lumber for building construction in Austin. In the fall of 1839 he sent a slave to Austin with a load of lumber and, on the

The site of the original White homestead just west of the Cedar Creek community in Bastrop County, Texas, off Highway 21. The house was located in the center of the photograph, just in front of the line of trees, and was burned around 1869. Photo taken by Donaly Brice in May, 1986.

return trip, the slave was shot and killed by a band of Indians. Life in Bastrop County was not always troublesome, however, and Hamilton II contributed to its brighter side. Horse racing was a popular pastime and in 1840 Hamilton II, as proprietor of the local race course, advertised in Austin's *Texas Sentinel* the upcoming three-day Bastrop Fall Races scheduled to commence on October 15.[2]

Hamilton II also held public office three times during the period of time Texas was a Republic. To serve in these positions he posted bond on the following dates: February 24, 1845 as Constable; August 13, 1846 as Justice of the Peace; and August 18, 1846 as Surveyor. In the spring of 1847, during the War with Mexico, he served for six weeks as a private in the Bastrop County Mounted Volunteer Company's expedition to San Antonio and was honorably discharged. Hamilton White II is considered one of the early pioneers of Texas.

Prior to 1867 Hamilton and Tabitha White had acquired a large amount of land between them, totaling 3,887 acres, with their first deed being registered on December 23, 1837. Four tracts of 320 acres each had been obtained by Patent under the Pre-emption (Homestead) Act of 1845. According to the 1860 census Hamilton II's Bastrop County land holdings amounted to $10,760 with personal property valued at $5,900. The Agricultural census for 1860 listed Hamilton II as owning 890 acres of land, 250 acres of which was improved acreage valued at six thousand dollars. Apparently the Whites found the buying and selling of land profitable for by 1867 they had sold 3,172 acres of their land. They were also slaveholders, owning five in 1850 and eleven in 1860. Hamilton White was alleged to be the second wealthiest man in Bastrop County.[3]

While living in Bastrop County seven additional children were born to the Whites: Celestia in 1837 who died before 1860; Virginia on January 13, 1843; Martha (Mattie) in 1845; Laura in 1848; Mary Hamilton (Mollie) on October 17, 1850; Hamilton III on April 17, 1854; and John on August 9, 1855.[4]

Young Ham White had the distinction of being born and raised in one of the twenty-three original counties of the Republic of Texas, which hosted the settlement of Stephen F. Austin's first colony in Texas in 1829. At that time Bastrop County contained all of fifteen present-day counties. In 1874, when White was twenty years old, the last boundary change occurred, reducing the county to its present size of 867 square miles. Until the early 1880s the county remained chiefly agricultural with cotton production, under a plantation system, as its main product. Approximately twelve miles east of White's homeplace grew the unusual forest called the "Lost Pines of Texas." This isolated stand of loblolly pines, so named because of its eighty-some mile separation from the eastern limit of the main pine belt, constituted Bastrop County's first commercial product, timber — used in many early buildings in central Texas.[5] Unlike many Texas children, Ham White had the pleasure of spending his youth either wandering the vast pine forest or scouting the spacious prairie to the west.

Until his early teens Ham grew up a typical west Texas boy. After four years of schooling he continued his education at home. It is evident that White was intelligent; apparently the limited education he received was not wasted, for later he demonstrated remarkable literacy skills for one so unschooled.[6]

As the eldest son and namesake, Ham was closely attached and devoted to his father, a man well respected and esteemed by the community. Ham was barely thirteen years of age when he was devastated by his father's tragic and brutal death.

At some point during the 1860s a dispute arose over hog range between Ham's father and a family named Rowe. Thomas Rowe and his wife Mary had been neighbors of the Whites since moving from South Carolina in 1846. Although the Rowes had several children only one son, James, figured prominently in the feud.[7] It reached a climax on Green's Creek during the evening of June 12, 1867. According to *The Houston Daily Telegraph*:

> We regret to announce that Mr. Ham White was killed on Wednesday evening last, on his return to his farm on Cedar Creek from the town of Bastrop. It appears that he had reached a small creek in the neighborhood of Mr. Alexander, some eight miles west of town, and had gotten out of his buggy to make an examination of the water to see whether it had swollen too much to prevent his crossing, when he was approached by some person or persons and shot through the head, the body, and the wrist. His body was discovered a very short time after the occurrence took place, by Mr. George Moore, who was returning to his home in the neighborhood where the occurrence took place, from town. We have learned that parties have already been suspicioned as connected with the affair, but we will not mention any names until facts are fully developed in the premises. Mr. White was an old resident of Bastrop County, and was well acquainted through this section. He leaves a large family to mourn his loss.[8]

On October 28, 1867 Tabitha White petitioned the Probate Court to appoint Commissioners to inventory and appraise her husband's estate. The petition was granted but the estate was not appraised so, on November 7, she petitioned for a reappointment of Commissioners. The inventory and appraisal were submitted and approved by the Probate Court on February 28, 1868. The inventory listed the following property belonging to the White estate: 440 acres of land; five horses; one mule; two hundred sheep; fifty head of cattle; forty hogs; seven yokes of oxen; two wagons and other miscellaneous property, with a total value of $1,860. All claims against the estate amounted to $125.[9]

The tragedy and aftermath of his father's death created an overpow-

Photograph of Ham White's sister, Martha "Mattie" White Murchison, circa 1890s. Furnished to author by Mrs. Laura Cunningham of Austin, Texas, great-niece of Ham White.

ering desire for revenge which so engulfed young Ham that it ultimately altered the course of his life, bringing about his criminal career. His devotion to and memory of his father's image would also emerge and clearly manifest itself when he attempted to add honor to his unhonorable deeds. In a newspaper interview years later, White described his feelings at the time:

> I, child as I was, over the bloody corpse of my murdered father, took a solemn oath to devote my whole life, if necessary, to avenge his death, and to kill his cowardly and treacherous assassin. This cold blooded, and as far as I knew unprovoked murder, changed me at once from the innocent confiding boy to an avenging Nemesis. My entire thought and objection in life appeared to be to meet and slay this man who had so abruptly despoiled our family. . . . My desire for vengeance appeared to "grow with my growth and strengthen with my strength." Nothing short of "an eye for an eye and a tooth for a tooth" would satisfy me. . . . Upon the day that I arrived at maturity I visited my father's grave, and there renewed my oath of vengeance, and vowed that ere another sun would set I would kill his murderer.

The object of White's wrath, and undoubtedly the slayer of his father, was twenty-seven-year-old James Rowe who left Bastrop County immediately after the killing and did not return for two years. He was never arrested for the murder and shortly after his return the White farmhouse mysteriously burned to the ground, forcing the White family to move to "the river farm" closer to the town of Bastrop. Ham's mother forbade him to return to the old homeplace for fear he would kill Rowe.[10] For the next eight years Ham White lived in a completely female-dominated household with thoughts of revenge festering in his mind.

In the summer of 1875 his pent-up emotions broke loose and the twenty-one-year-old White committed his first crime. Around August 6 he stole a herd of cattle in Caldwell County and drove them north. An indictment was issued from Bastrop County for which bond was immediately paid, likely by his mother. Six additional indictments for cattle theft were issued on December 1. In late September he was captured in Milam County and incarcerated in the Rockdale jail. A few days later he was turned over to a Milam County deputy sheriff for return to Caldwell County.[11] According to *The Daily Democratic Statesman*:

Site of the murder of Ham White's father, Hamilton White II, on Greens Creek in Bastrop County, Texas. The murder occurred on June 12, 1867. Photo taken by Donaly Brice in May, 1986.

Just before leaving Rockdale the deputy and prisoner were walking about the town when, coming to a hardware store, White asked if he might go in and buy a knife. The request was granted and the deputy stood at the door. The knives were in the back way, and while there White discovered a pistol (his real object) and asked what it was worth. The clerk of the store replied twenty-five dollars. White then said, "If you will put six cartridges in it I will give you thirty." The clerk being innocent of whom he was said, "all right," and the pistol was loaded. White of course bought the knife and came with it open towards the deputy. Now comes a change over the spirit of the deputy's dream. They had gone about four miles from town, when the deputy got down to get water at a spring, he looked up and there was a pistol in his face. He caved. White escaped. . . .[12]

The White family cemetery near Cedar Creek, Bastrop County, Texas. Large tomb-
stone marks the grave of Ham White's brother, John White. The cemetery is located
just east of the old homestead. Photo taken by Donaly Brice in May, 1986.

Now a fugitive, White set out with determination to fulfill his vow
of vengeance and made his way back to Bastrop County. At dusk on
October 7 he rode to a spot near the Rowe house and waited patiently
for James Rowe to appear.

According to White's version, as soon as he saw Rowe he started
walking toward him. Sighting his adversary, Rowe began running in
the opposite direction. Continuing to advance toward Rowe, and
knowing he was armed, White ordered him to defend himself. Ignoring the command Rowe continued running. White then opened fire
with his revolver, his first shot breaking Rowe's right arm. The next
shot entered Rowe's back and came out his throat, immediately killing
him. On hearing the gunshots James' younger brother, thirty-two-
year-old Alexander, rushed to the scene and began firing at his broth-

11

er's killer. Rowe fired eight times, wounding him in several places. White held no animosity toward Alexander and refused to return his fire. Seeing that his horse had been killed, White painfully hobbled away from the scene of conflict.[13]

The Bastrop Advertiser and *The Daily Democratic Statesman* in Austin, however, gave a somewhat different version of Rowe's killing:

The Bastrop Advertiser.

ANOTHER MURDER — Just as we go to press we learn of another horrible murder which occurred on Cedar Creek, 12 miles west of Bastrop, on Thursday evening. The particulars as we got them from Mr. Norgrath, one of the jury of inquest, are that about dark Thursday evening, while Mr. Jas. V. Rhoe [*sic*], was in his lot feeding his horse, a man rode up to the fence and began shooting at him with a Spencer rifle. Mr. Rhoe, in the effort to evade the shots, ran around the corn crib, the man all the while continuing to shoot at him. He finally got into the crib, as he thought for security, where he was shot to death, no less than twelve or fifteen shots being fired at him. We are told that Rhoe called lustily for his six-shooter, but there being no one at the house, or in hearing, but his aged mother, it was not carried to him. The jury of inquest fail to elicit any evidence [as] to the murder, though strong [feeling] amounting to almost certainty exist among the people as to who did the deed. As usual, as of date, the murderer escaped.

The Daily Democratic Statesman:

Two travelers from Colorado county, who arrived in this city yesterday, report that on Tuesday [*sic*] evening a man named James Rowe was killed while at work at a corn crib by an unknown assassin. Rowe was shot five times, the last ball passing thorugh his neck and causing instant death.

Since writing the above as we are informed by Mr. J.J. Allen of this city that a boy named Ham White was supposed to have done the killing, as he swore he would kill Rowe, who had killed the boy's father twelve years ago.[14]

Basically, White's account and the newspaper's version agree that White shot Rowe as he was trying to get away. The major difference was that White failed to point out that the killing took place in a corn crib. As neither newspaper mentioned the shooting of White by Rowe's brother, evidently the Rowe family did not report it. By March of 1877 the *Daily Democratic Statesman* had obtained all the details of the killing and gave the following report: "Ham White, the notorious highwayman, now in jail, has one stiff knee, caused by a shot from the brother of the man Rowe, who was killed by White about a year ago. . . ."[15]

After killing Rowe, White laboriously managed to reach the home of a local doctor who dressed his wounds. That night he obtained another horse and rode forty miles to San Marcos where he remained under a Doctor Denton's care for several months.

White finally had gotten his revenge although he had paid a high price. He sustained a serious wound to his right knee, rendering it stiff and unresilient and leaving him with a decided limp. Not only a painful reminder, this telltale limp became a major mark of identification that would plague him for life.[16]

On October 12 Governor Richard Coke issued a Governor's Proclamation offering two hundred dollars for the arrest of "Hamey" White for the murder of James Rowe.[17]

The next day the Rowe family inserted the following reward in Austin's *Daily Democratic Statesman*:

$500 Reward

Murdered!

On the seventh day of October, 1875, James Rowe, resident of Bastrop County, by Ham White. Anyone delivering the said person inside the jail of Bastrop or Travis Counties will be paid the above reward. The Governor also offers $200.

Description of Said White

Height — five feet, ten or eleven inches; weight — 165 or 170 pounds; age — twenty or twenty-one years; color of hair — dark, though not black; complexion — dark; face large and round, with no mustache or whiskers; eyes — light blue or grey, and very large; stands erect and straight.

Alexander Rowe
Horace Rowe[18]

Lending evidence that White was not lame previous to the Rowe fight, this reward stated White "stands erect and straight" while the Governor's Proclamation reported "he stands erect and is very stout."

On December 1, 1875 White was indicted for the Rowe murder in Bastrop County. On December 3 his bond for cattle theft was forfeited and the court ordered that he be found and brought back to Bastrop County and jailed.[19]

Apparently the killing of Rowe purged all resentment White had harbored and for seventeen months he committed no crime. He regained his strength after several months of recovery and, realizing his freedom would be short-lived if he remained in the area much longer, proceeded to execute a plan of action. Using the last of his money to hire three men and purchase a team and wagon, White headed west to hunt buffalo. Leaving civilization behind, his party reached the headwaters of the Colorado River in west Texas and made camp approximately one hundred miles from the nearest habitation.[20]

By 1874 the great herds of buffalo had moved south from the Kansas plains through the panhandle into west Texas. The location of these herds were soon discovered by buffalo hunter J. Wright Mooar who reported his find to other hunters around Dodge City. The hunters, in turn, left for west Texas and headquartered out of Fort Griffin. In 1876 the dealers in hides and hunters' supplies followed the hunters to Fort Griffin, which became the foremost frontier hide market. But, by 1878 this immense buffalo herd had been decimated almost to the point of extinction.[21] It was during the peak year of 1876 that White and his crew arrived, set up camp and began hunting buffalo. White later claimed this was the happiest period of his life. It ended one Saturday evening in mid-December of 1876.

Gathered around the campfire and planning a trip to Fort Griffin the next morning, White's attention was diverted by a signal from one of the men on lookout on a high peak nearby. Ascending the peak, White observed a large party of men heading for their camp. He immediately realized they were not Indians but Texas rangers. Returning quickly to the campsite, he saddled his horse and instructed the men to take his belongings to the Fort, sell the hides, and keep the money until he could pick it up. By this time the rangers had almost reached the camp and began firing at White as he sped away. Being better mounted he succeeded in losing his pursuers after a harrowing chase of about a mile.

Apparently White remained in the area for some time trying to obtain his money. Unsuccessful, he made his way to the home of a friend in Brown County and arranged for the man to go to the Fort and collect his money and possessions. After several days the man returned, stating that the hunters would not release the property without

Hamey White.   Reward.

Proclamation

By the Governor of the State of Texas

$200 Reward

To all to whom these presents shall come

Whereas it has been made known to me that on the 7th day of October 1875 in the county of Bastrop, State of Texas, Hamey White did murder James Rowe, and that said murderer is still at large, and a fugitive from justice.

Now therefore I Richard Coke Governor of Texas do, by virtue of the authority vested in me by the constitution and laws of this State, hereby offer a reward of two hundred dollars for the arrest and delivery of the said Hamey White to the Sheriff of Bastrop County inside the jail door of said County.

In testimony whereof I have hereto signed my name and caused the Great Seal of State to be affixed at the City of Austin this the 12th day of October A.D. 1875

(Signed) Richd Coke
Governor

(L. S.)

By the Governor

(Signed) A. W. DeBerry
Secretary of State

Description - - - - - - - - - - - Hamey White is five feet ten or eleven inches high, weight about 145 pounds, is 20 or 21 years old, has dark hair, dark complexion, large round face, has no whiskers or moustache, has very large blue or gray eyes. He stands erect and is very stout.

15

written authorization. At White's insistence the man reluctantly agreed to return to Fort Griffin for White's property. The next morning the Brown County man asked White to accompany him to a neighbor's house, promising to leave from there and return to the Fort. As the pair traveled the road to the nearby house, six men with revolvers emerged from the brush and captured White. Evidently the "friend" had learned about the rewards and decided to lead White into a trap.

With White secured, his captors started out for Bastrop. About four miles from Brownwood, White's horse gave a sudden start. Taking advantage of the situation he threw himself on the side of the horse Comanche fashion and, under a hail of bullets, succeeded in outrunning his pursuers.

Not having seen or heard from his family in over a year, White decided to return to Bastrop County. Being without funds, he made his way to the home of a friend named Stephen Brimley near Brownwood who furnished him with five dollars and a revolver.

White immediately set out for home unaware that in a few days his career as a stagecoach robber would begin. He traveled eastward for four days. Then, on March 6, 1877, he chanced on the stopped stagecoach between Waco and Gatesville, observed the affluent passengers and formulated his plans. The following morning he robbed his first stagecoach.[22]

The Pardon of This Young Man Will Be The Restoration To The World of One Whose Manly Qualifications Will Lead Him To Pursue Thenceforth an Honorable Career

The last thing on the mind of the stage driver from Waco on the morning of March 7, 1877 was stage robbery. As the horses strained against their traces to haul the lagging stage up the incline, the driver caught sight of a man mounted on a bay horse on the crest of the hill. When the coach reached the top, Ham White suddenly wrenched his horse around. The startled driver froze as he peered down the barrel of a six-shooter and heard the command to halt.

The stage carried one female and six male passengers. White, ordering the men out of the coach, remarked that he was too much of a gallant to rob a lady and allowed her to remain seated. One passenger, a youth from Tennessee, after handing over one hundred dollars told White that he was a poor man and this money was all he had. White returned twenty dollars and promised that he would in the future return the full amount. White later stated that he "deplored the robbery of this youth, more than any other."

As he gathered their valuables, the jovial bandit bantered with the passengers and soon had them joking in return. He then ordered the driver to open the mail pouch, quipping that he was now an accomplice in robbing the U.S. mails. White, who had remained mounted during the entire robbery, bid the passengers goodbye and after receiving a pleasant goodbye in return, rode off. Once out of sight of the stage he opened the registered letters. In addition to the $160 he had obtained from the passengers, he took twenty dollars and a quantity of postage stamps from the mail. He then rode to Comanche Springs and hid out for two days at the home of a friend named Christy.[1]

With money now jingling in his pocket, White continued to Bastrop County. In his own words: "Here every person in the place had known me all my life. My object in visiting the town was to have a race with the officers with the determination of killing every one of them if I could, so completely hardened I had become."

After visiting about a week, he left home and headed north with his mind filled with visions of robbing stagecoaches. Following his initial holdup, White's career as a highwayman was fast and furious. It became an obsession with him and during a nineteen-day period he robbed a total of five stagecoaches.

On March 19 White made his second strike, stopping the stage between Georgetown and Salado. As the stage carried no passengers or cargo, he gained nothing and dejectedly returned to Bastrop County.[2]

Cedar Creek residents had known and liked White from childhood and, although he was wanted for Rowe's murder, they did not report him to the authorities. During White's visits his mother made clothes for him and sewed money in the cuffs of his pants. However, not all of his relatives were so taken with him. His sister, Laura Murchison, would not allow her children to mention his name and would spank any child who did. Nevertheless, her two eldest sons, Eugene and Walter, were fond of their uncle and would slip out and meet him in the cemetery. After this last short visit, White bid his family goodbye without informing anyone of his plans.[3]

On March 23 White held up the McDade-Bastrop stage six miles outside of Bastrop. Overtaking the stagecoach from the rear, he caught the driver, Junius Nash, by surprise and demanded his surrender. The driver immediately stopped the stage which contained three men and one woman. Again White remained in the saddle, made the men get out, and told the woman he would not rob or harm her. After collecting the passengers' money and valuables he waved the coach on. Realizing that he had neglected to get the mail pouch, he caught up with the coach and stopped it again, commanding the driver to cut the pouch and give him the contents. It was a disappointing robbery for White who gained only eleven dollars from a passenger named Chester Erehart and nothing but letters from the mail pouch. He then rode to the home of a friend name Donnehue where he remained for the next two days.[4]

On March 26 White added something new to his bag of tricks by robbing two stages in one day. During the morning he stopped the stage from Austin to Lockhart driven by James Browder. As in his previous robberies, he made the four passengers get out of the coach and then robbed them. Stating that he did not rob laboring men, White gave back twenty dollars he had taken from passenger James Burt because he noticed his calloused hands. He collected eighty dollars from the other three passengers and, after rifling the mail of twelve dollars, allowed the stage to proceed to Lockhart.[5]

At three o'clock that afternoon White halted the Austin to San Antonio stage three miles north of the Blanco River. First he directed the driver, James Conley, to pull off the road but quickly changed his mind and told him to stop in the road. He then ordered the two passengers out of the coach. John Corbin from Baltimore surrendered fifty-four dollars and his watch but White gave an elderly German his ten dollars back, remarking: "You look like you work hard for your money, and so I will let you keep that."

Turning to the driver, White ordered him to throw down the mail bags. At first the man refused, stating that the action would violate his oath. Pointing his revolver at Conley, the bandit said in a halfway joshing tone, "This is the oath you will obey." Immediately the four mail sacks were thrown down. Remaining in his saddle, he commanded the passenger Corbin to cut each sack open and keep its contents separate as he did not want to inconvenience the government. The last sack contained registered mail and White, using his left hand, took it from Corbin, tore the largest letter open with his teeth and extracted a wad of greenbacks. Pleased with his success, he told Corbin, "As I have done so well, I'll give you back your watch and chain," and then ordered him to replace the mail and throw the pouches back on the stage. As the bandit rode off he boasted, "This is the second stage I've gone through today." He had finally scored. Besides the fifty-four dollars from Corbin, he pocketed one thousand dollars from the U.S. Mail pouch.[6]

With money in his pocket at last, White headed east toward Lockhart where the next day he met a friend from Mountain City in Hays County named John Vaughn. White and twenty-one-year-old Vaughn headed for Luling in southern Caldwell County. Stabling their horses, the two went on a spending spree, buying clothing and liberally spreading money all over town.[7] White's obvious lack of discretion soon came to the attention of his old nemesis, the Texas rangers.

During this period of the late 1870s the rangers were considered the most efficient law enforcement agency in Texas. The term "ranger" was first applied to a fighting group in 1823 but the organization did not receive legal status until the Texas Revolution in 1835. Prior to the Civil War the rangers' main duties were controlling the Comanche Indians and patrolling the border between Texas and Mexico for marauding Mexican bandits. Throughout the Civil War the rangers were in abeyance; during the following nine years of Reconstruction misrule they were replaced by Governor E.J. Davis' hated State Police.

Defeating Davis for the Governorship of Texas during the election of 1873, Governor Richard Coke turned his attention to the lawless situation in Texas. Although the western settlements were still threatened by Indian attacks the major problems were organized gangs of outlaws and bloody feudists that carried on their own private wars. Texas never needed the rangers more than it did at this time and, through legislative action, two bodies of fighting forces were organized in May of 1874: the Frontier Battalion, consisting of six companies, was placed under the command of Major John B. Hall; the Special Forces came under the charge of Captain Leander H. McNelly. It was this latter force that would deal with White.[8]

Receiving news of the stage robberies, Lieutenant Lee Hall and Rangers McMurray, Pendleton, and Allen started in pursuit of the bandit. Leaving Austin at 2 AM on the twenty-seventh, they rode to the site of the San Antonio-Austin stage robbery. Here they gathered up post office bills giving the particulars of registered money letters. Finding the trail of the bandit's horse they followed it in the direction of Lockhart. After four or five miles they lost the trail but were able to keep on the track by requesting information about a man riding a good bay horse. *The Daily Democratic Statesman* reported what followed:

> About 12 p.m. Wednesday they arrived in Luling and stopped at a livery stable to feed their jaded animals, and as they dismounted they noticed a man in the same stable saddling a bay horse, and the moment they looked at him sharply he appeared nervous and uneasy. Lieut. Hall then entered conversation with him and as he gradually drew near, the man began to give back and finally said, "Don't come near me," raising his hand towards the inside of his coat. Lieut. Hall said, "Why, you appear frightened," and he replied that "it is enough to frighten anyone to be surrounded by three or four men." At this moment the three rangers, who were off a few steps, drew their pistols and the Lieutenant seized the man by the wrist, the others closing in and disarming and searching

Blank No. 1.

THE WESTERN UNION TELEGRAPH COMPANY.

This Company **TRANSMITS** and **DELIVERS** messages only on conditions, limiting its liability, which have been assented to by the sender of the following message.
Errors can be guarded against only by repeating a message back to the sending station for comparison, and the Company will not hold itself liable for errors or delays in transmission or delivery of **Unrepeated Messages.**
This message is an **UNREPEATED MESSAGE**, and delivered by request of the sender under the conditions named above.

A. R. BREWER, Sec'y.   WILLIAM ORTON, Pres't.

Dated _Luling_ X 2 8 187 7

Received at _Austin Meh 28_

To _Gen Wm Steele_

Have captured the stage
robber & most of
the money — will be
in Austin tomorrow

J F Hall

15 Collect

READ THE NOTICE AT THE TOP.

(29)

him. Inside his coat, next to his breast, a six shooter was found, and from his pocket $320 in $20 bills was taken. His saddlebags were then searched and an old dirty shirt, $570 was found in an old dirty sock, and the packages of money and the amounts exactly corresponded with the numbers given in the post office bills picked up where the robbery occurred. This man proved to be Ham White. . . ."[9]

Posing as brothers, White and Vaughn had become conspicuous around Luling as a result of their numerous inquiries about the stage schedules. This prompted several of the townspeople to ask the rangers if they were going to arrest White's brother. The rangers had heard nothing of White's companion and when the citizens pointed him out, they quickly arrested him. Vaughn insisted that he did not know White but that he had traveled with him from Lockhart. In his coat the rangers found $111 in two dollar bills and asked where he got it. Vaughn told them it was none of their business.

The rangers took their two prisoners thirteen miles north to Lockhart. Before locking them in the jail for the night they found and removed several steel saws that were tied to White's legs. The next morning Vaughn told the rangers he had borrowed the money from White and had nothing to do with the robberies. According to *The Daily Democratic Statesman*, when asked by the officers why he had hung around the area instead of escaping after the robberies, White replied that "it was no use in a man tearing himself all to pieces in the brush after he had made a good haul." *The Daily Express*, however, reported that the bandit did plan to leave: "Says that he was about to leave Texas for Indiana, where he wanted to have his leg treated."

An incriminating journal found on White stated:

March 7 — If I am killed today, bury me quietly and do not give my description. H.W.B.

March 19 — Danger today. As you have killed me, do as you please. Ham

March 19 — Came empty.

March 23 — I will try the Bastrop line today. H.W.B.

March 26 — I don't think there is much danger this morning, but a great deal this evening.

Ham[10]

On March 29 the rangers brought the two prisoners to Austin. As news of White's arrival spread, people lined the streets to get a glimpse

No 593

Recorded

United States

Robbin u.s
mail from
Austin to Fort
Griffin.

Harm White —

Indictment:

U.S. Wit
    James E Browder
            S. Dis Austin
James Burks   "
Lee Hall   State from
P.m. — — Austin —

Filed April 12. 1877
M. Hopkins

of the now notorious outlaw. That evening the rangers turned White and Vaughn over to the Federal Authorities. As a result of the capture the rangers earned a $1,200 reward offered by Bastrop County plus an additional bonus of fifty dollars from U.S. Marshall Thomas Purnell.[11]

For the second time in as many months White had been betrayed by a friend. Vaughn's disassociation with him and his denial of their friendship profoundly affected him. From this point on White became a solitudinous figure, associating with no one and trusting only himself. Consequently, he gained his notorious sobriquet, "the lone highwayman."

The two prisoners remained in jail until April 12 when the grand jury found three indictments against White for robbing the United States mails and three against Vaughn as an accessory in the San Antonio-Austin stage robbery. White's trial began the next day, Friday, April 13, in United States District Court at Austin under Judge Thomas Duval. Attorney A.J. Evans represented the prosecution but W.M. Walton, who had represented White during his preliminary examination after he was brought to Austin, withdrew from the defense. The next day the court appointed Attorney H.S. Bentley as defense counsel.

On Monday, April 16, White pled not guilty. Nonetheless, after a short deliberation, the jury found him guilty on all three charges the same day. *The Daily Democratic Statesman* made this observation: "White wept when his counsel, Mr. Bentley, alluded to the grief of a mother, and he seemed overcome and cast down." On April 19, Judge Duval sentenced White to serve a life term at hard labor at the West Virginia State Penitentiary at Moundsville.[12]

John Vaughn's case was called on the seventeenth and continued until the next court term. On July 18, 1877 the case against John Vaughn was resumed and on the nineteenth he was found not guilty.[13]

About April 23 White, chained and well guarded, was taken to the photographic gallery of H.R. Marks on Congress Street in Austin. The Lampasas *Dispatch* graphically described what transpired:

> Ham White wore a sad, dejected face . . . He never quailed, even when he sat in the gallery of the artist Marks that perfect representations of his strong vigorous face may adorn the walls of the rogues' galleries of the world.[14]

On April 26 United States Marshal Thomas Purnell took White

Although there is no documentation to confirm authenticity, it is very probable that this photograph, titled unidentified biography in the H.R. Marks photographic collection at the Austin History Center, Austin, Texas Public Library, is the photograph of Ham White taken in late April, 1877. During the fall of 1987, the North Carolina State Bureau of Investigation in Raleigh compared this photograph to White's San Quentin photograph taken in 1891. Although it is impossible to state positively that both photographs were of the same man, Mr. John Neuner of the latent evidence division wrote to the author on November 17, 1987, "As an untrained observer, a consistency in the bone structure of the face is apparent."

into custody for deliverance to the West Virginia Penitentiary. Taking no chances, Purnell searched his prisoner and found an iron bar White had concealed in his pants leg to facilitate his escape. Wild rumors concerning a rescue attempt reached Purnell and, although unfounded, he took precautionary measures. According to the Lampassas *Dispatch*:

> Thieves and robbers of the West sold, it is stated, 6000 head of stolen cattle to raise a fund to defend or rescue White. The United States Marshals are advised of this fact, and five armed men and twice as many repeaters and an equal number of Winchester rifles are trained upon White . . . He was told by the Deputy Marshal, when he was getting on the train, that he would be shot the very instant the train was assailed, or whenever he made an effort to escape.

Needless to say, no adverse incidents occurred during the trip and the marshal had no trouble delivering White to the authorities at the penitentiary on May 1.[15]

White's conduct in prison, for the most part, was exemplary, committing only minor infractions which he confessed with candor. Basically he followed the rules, set an example for other prisoners and gained the confidence of the entire prison staff. Placed at work in the prison carriage shop, White earned a considerable amount of money in overtime. He made himself popular with Superintendent W.L. Bridges and other prison officials and became a show prisoner whom prison visitors wished to see.

On July 1, 1879 White began his quest for a pardon by writing President Rutherford B. Hayes. In August, 1879, with complete confidence in White's reformation, Superintendent Bridges wrote Judge Alexander T. Gray of the Department of Justice in Washington, D.C. praising White and setting in motion a petition for his pardon. By February, 1881, with help from the officials of the West Virginia Penitentiary, he had gained the support of Judge Gray, District Judge Thomas Duval who had tried White in Austin, U.S. Attorney A.J. Evans who prosecuted him, West Virginia Governor Henry Matthews, Texas Congressman George Washington Jones, and U.S. Attorney General Charles Deours. In addition, a majority of the citizens in and around Bastrop County sent a pardon petition of fifty-one legal-size pages of signatures to President Hayes.

The pardon petition had been signed by at least twenty prominent

Moundsville W. Va
July 1st 1879

Washington D. C

President Hays

Dear sir

It is with a sad heart that
I write this letter to you hardly
hopinge that it will be answered. I am a convic under a
life sentence, for highway robery
committed in Texas, this is my
3rd year impusonment, am
now 25 years old. I will make
no excuse for my crimes for it
would take too much space
I wish to ask you a few questions, as I have no lawyer to ad-
vise me, nor no money to emply
one. Has Hon J. W. Jones made
any effort in my behalf
Would a petition for me or pardon
don sined by all or nearly all

the county officers and one
hundred of the leading citizen
of the county that I was raised
in (and where the principal part
of my develment was done) and th
co paper with an artical show
ing that they were such. be
surficient to secure me a pard
provided the N.S. judge that
I was tried before, and prosecute
ing atty recomended it
I ask you to answer this for my
Mothers sake who is far away doin
all she can for her wayward boy
I beleave if you knew the grea
crime that caused her to
be a widow and me a fatha
-less boy when I was only (11) eleven
years of age, and in after years
to be an outlaw; and at
last, to occupy a felons cel

that you would an-
swer this letter. I have but one
true friend in this wide world
and she is 70 years old if she
should die while I am in
heare my only hope is gone
Respectfully
Ham White

P.S. Address in care
W. L. Bridges Supt
Moundsville
W. Va

W. L. Bridges, Eq.,
Supt Pen'y,
Moundsville,
W. Va.

Please state what you
know about this man's case.
Very Resp'y
R. F. Gray,
Dept Justice

.EXECUTIVE MANSION,
WASHINGTON.

7 Feb. 1881

Mr sclgp Gray:

Please give this

Case Early attention.

RB Hayes

officials from the town and county of Bastrop as well as jury foreman John W. Glenn and several jury members who convicted him, and Chester Erehart, White's robbery victim on the Bastrop stage. The residents in and around Bastrop County, if not condoning the Rowe killing at least felt White was justified and that his stage robberies resulted from his frustration over what he considered an injustice. However, the murder charge against White remained active but all charges of cattle theft were dropped on October 20, 1879.[16]

On February 7, 1881 President Hayes wrote the following note to Judge Gray regarding White's pardon: "Judge Gray. Please give this case early attention. R.B. Hayes."

In a letter dated February 22, 1881 to Attorney General Deours, Judge Gray had this to say: "I am convinced that the pardon of this young man will be the restoration to the world of one whose manly qualifications will lead him to pursue thenceforth an honorable career."[17]

White's hometown newspaper, *The Bastrop Advertiser*, followed these proceedings with great interest, lending their support to White's cause. An article in *The Galveston Daily News*, which offended the *Advertiser*, stated: ". . . . possibly president Garfield is not aware that there is really no reason to send reinforcements to Texas stage robbers"; and "Congressman [George Washington] Jones was not sent to Washington to dram up recruits for the road agents and in doing so he is possibly carrying his independence too far." The *Advertiser* rebutted: ". . . The News does Col. Jones a gross injustice, and one it should have the manliness to correct. While we differ politically with Col. Jones, we cannot approve of such slanderous modes of attack."[18] As for White, the *Advertiser* stated, ". . . he is of such disposition and traits of character that, if released, he would become a good citizen. . . . and to assert its belief that Ham White is a changed man and will make a good citizen."[19]

On March 1, through executive action, White received a pardon as one of Hayes' last acts as President.[20] A rumor that circulated later claimed that White had received a Presidential pardon because he was a "near relative" of Secretary of the Navy Goff.[21] None of the newspaper reports or correspondence to the President included in the pardon file alludes to this in any manner. *The Bastrop Advertiser* printed the following complete copy of White's pardon which clearly outlines the grounds on which it was granted:

RUTHERFORD B. HAYES
President of the U.S. of America

To all to whom these Presents shall come — Greetings:

Whereas, Hamilton White, otherwise called Ham White, on conviction of robbing the U.S. Mail on the highway, was sentenced by U.S. District Court for the Western District of Texas on the 19th day of April 1877 to imprisonment for life in the West Virginia Penitentiary, and whereas, his pardon is earnestly prayed for by a very large number of the citizens of Bastrop County in Texas and by his aged and respected mother.

And whereas, the late Judge Duvall [*sic*] who presided at his trial —appears by a letter of the Judges addressed to the prisoner and filed with the application for pardon, was disposed to recommend at the proper time, executive clemency.

And whereas, the U.S. Attorney for said District now recommends pardon.

And whereas, the offenses of said White were committed when he was only 21 years old, and the peculiar circumstance under which the same were committed may properly be taken into consideration in his behalf.

And whereas, it is credibly represented to me that he is of such disposition and traits of character that, if released, he will become a good citizen.

Now therefore, be it known, that I, Rutherford B. Hayes, President of the United States of America, in consideration of the premises, divers other good and sufficient reasons me to moving, so hereby grant to the said Hamilton White, otherwise called Ham White a full and unconditioned pardon.

In testimony whereof I have hereinto signed my signature and the seal of the United States to be affixed.

Done at the City of Washington, this first day of March A.D. 1881 and of the Independence of the United States.

R. B. Hayes

By the President:
Wm. M. Evans, Secretary of State[22]

On March 8 Superintendent Bridges received the warrant for pardon. Giving White his release pay of five dollars, Bridges discharged him on the same day.[23]

White left the West Virginia Penitentiary not quite a hero but likely a slightly tarnished one to those who supported him in Bastrop County.

Department of Justice,

Washington, *March 5*, 1881

To

Sup't West Virginia Pen'y,
            Moundsville, W. Va. :

Sir:

Herewith receive Warrant for Pardon of Hamilton White, otherwise called *Ham White*

which please deliver to *him*, and report RELEASE to this Department, retaining this letter as your authority.

By direction of the Attorney General:

Alexander J. Gray,

Clerk Pardons

(OVER.)

33

PART II

The Lone Hand

CHAPTER THREE

We Don't Rob Ladies — We Don't Rob Cripples

On March 26, 1881 Ham White came home with the support of most of the population of Bastrop County and a Presidential pardon in his pocket. Handshakes and words of encouragement from old friends and well-wishers gave him a sense of pride and jubilance. In all fairness to White, he quite possibly intended to reform but in a week's time any future hopes and plans were shattered. On the night of April 2 Bastrop County Sheriff William E. Jenkins arrested him for the 1875 murder of James Rowe.

White engaged the services of Major J.D. Sayers and Col. George Washington Jones as defense counsel. On April 8 the attorneys filed White's application for writ of habeas corpus before Judge Moore in District Court at Lockhart and he was released on $2,500 bond. On April 25, in District Court at Bastrop, the state of Texas continued his case for lack of evidence. In late April, unwilling to cope with another trial and possible prison term, White jumped bail and left Bastrop County heading due south.[1]

Feelings of disillusionment and resentment enveloped White and, using them as an excuse, he again turned to stagecoach robbery. His initial attempt occurred about May 1 near Gonzales, Texas. Approaching his quarry, White pulled his revolver and ordered the stagecoach to stop. The resolute driver, refusing to halt, left the chagrined bandit following in his wake futilely pointing his six-shooter at the stage. Not wanting to kill or hurt anyone, White reluctantly let the stage continue on.[2]

From this point White shifted his direction and headed north, robbing stages along his route. His next venture, although slightly more successful, still left him with little monetary gain. On the night of May 11 he stopped the Georgetown and Lampasas stage on Mesquite Creek, thirty-six miles southeast of Lampasas. The stage contained only two passengers, a man named Nixon from Austin and Flatonia stockman L.G. Robinson. White robbed them both, taking fifteen dollars from Nixon and forty dollars from Robinson. He allowed the stage to proceed to Lampasas after taking the mail bag but, finding nothing of value, he discarded it about three hundred yards from the robbery site where most of it was found the next morning.[3]

With this paltry amount to show for his efforts, White continued northward where his next robbery proved even less fruitful. Around ten o'clock on the morning of May 26, with his face blackened to hide his features, he stopped the Gatesville-Purmela stage approximately three miles east of Purmela. Ripping open the mail pouch, he removed two registered parcels and accidentally broke open a bag of needles which scattered inside the pouch. To his dismay he found only two womens' breast pens and sleeve buttons worth fifty cents. Again disappointed with a meager haul, he allowed the stage to resume its course to Purmela.[4]

On June 3, over one hundred and fifty miles to the north, White struck again with much better results. According to *The Galveston Daily News*:

> Gainesville, June 10 — Last Friday evening the stage of the Overland Transfer Company was robbed while passing through a place called Blair's Hollow, thirteen miles from Gainesville, by a masked man. He got very little money from the three passengers, but got $1,000 from the mail bags. W.E. Smith, mail agent, yesterday arrested W.R. Brown, a well-known stockman of Montague County, at Montague, and arrived here with him last night, and will take him to Denison tomorrow. Public sentiment as to Brown's guilt is about equally divided.

White later admitted to a *Denver Tribune* reporter that he committed this robbery as well as the attempted stage robbery near Gonzales and the holdup of the Georgetown and Lampasas stage. He also told the reporter that he committed the Gainesville robbery alone and that the man arrested for it was innocent.[5]

At this point White adopted the assumed name of Henry W. Burton, the first of several aliases he would use throughout his career. Although he was known only by these assumed names during the latter period of his life, for continuity and to avoid confusion he will be referred to as Ham White throughout the book.

After the Gainesville robbery White left Texas, continuing his trek north to Arkansas where he committed one of the most audacious hold-ups in the annals of western outlawry. Alone and unaided he robbed two stagecoaches simultaneously. He arrived in Fayetteville, Arkansas on June 14 and undoubtedly studied the stage routes during his journey. On the evening of the fifteenth he traveled to one of the loneliest locations on the road between Fayetteville and Alma. About five miles south of Mountainsburg he picked a post situated between two mountains and waited for the stage to arrive.

At 11 PM, armed with a revolver, White stopped the driver of the northbound stage. On command to get off the stagecoach, the driver and passengers quickly alighted only to be bound and blindfolded by the bandit. Placing the driver in front of the team with a warning that if he moved he was a dead man, he proceeded to rob the passengers of around thirty dollars and rifle the mail. The driver then asked White to loosen the strap on his wrists as it was causing him pain. He replied that he would as soon as he robbed the approaching southbound stage.

Halting the second stage, White ordered the driver and one passenger, H.D. Gray of Fayetteville, to get down. After binding and blindfolding the two men, he took five dollars and a silver watch and chain from Gray. He quickly located the mail sack, cut it open and removed all the valuables and registered letters. The take from the mail pouches from both stages was eighty-five dollars. For some unknown reason White then untied one of the passengers, warned him not to move or he would be killed, and disappeared into the woods heading east.

The passengers, fearing death, stood in the road blindfolded for ten minutes. By this time the driver of the northbound stage had worked his hands loose. Removing the blindfold and discovering that White had gone, he unbound the other victims. The relieved but shaken passengers boarded the stages and proceeded to their separate destinations.[6]

White wasted no time in making tracks out of Arkansas and headed for Colorado, recording his route in a pocket diary.

June 14 — Fayetteville, Arkansas
June 16 — Pearce City, Missouri, Decatur House

No. 72522-B

OFFICE OF

Post Office Inspector,

Denver, Colorado, Sept 28, 1881

David B. Parker
Chief Inspector
Washington D.C.

Dear Sir,

When H. M. Burton the mail robber who perpetrated the robbery of U.S. Mail between Alma and Fayetteville Ark. June 10/81, was captured at Pueblo Colo. June 29/81, after the robbery of the mail coach near Alamosa Colo. June 28/81, there was found on his person a heavy silver watch, and gold plated chain, which is claimed by one of the passengers on the mail coach when robbed by Burton in Ark. This watch has been accurately described to me in a letter by the alleged owner and is now in my possession.

June 17 — Wichita, Kansas
June 21 — South Arkansas
June 23 — Alpine. "I don't know whether it was a jail or hotel I stopped at."
June 24 — Pitkin, Pitkin House
June 25 — Gunnison City, Tabor House
June 26 — Lake City, American House
June 27 — Alamosa, Perry House.[7]

Following White's itinerary it is obvious that after entering Colorado he traveled on a Barlow-Sanderson stagecoach as all the towns listed were stage stops on this line. It is also evident that he used the stage line to study the routes, enabling him to pick the best location to commit a robbery. From his humorous entry of June 23 he must have lodged in a real fleabag at Alpine.

On June 25, during White's jaunt through Colorado, Deputy Postal Inspector L. Cass Carpenter in Denver received telegrams from Arkansas requesting the arrest of a man named H.M. Bourton [*sic*] for the robbery of the Alma-Fayetteville stagecoaches. The telegrams, besides offering a four hundred dollar reward for his capture, gave the

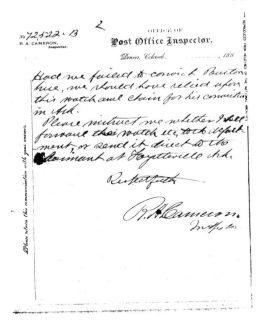

robber's description and stated that he was on his way through Pueblo to Denver and Cheyenne. Carpenter was unable to locate the bandit in Denver and on the twenty-seventh he departed for Cheyenne, hoping to intercept him. Failing to find his quarry there, he returned to Denver on the twenty-eighth.[8]

On the same day that Carpenter returned to Denver, White, wearing a linen duster and carrying a small bundle under his arm, entered Wilkins Livery Stable in Alamosa. After a few moments of pleasant conversation with liveryman P.W. Johnson, White hired a horse on the pretense of looking over the area for a prospective hay ranch. Leaving a deposit of eighty dollars, he rode directly to a site he had previously picked out about nine miles west of Alamosa.

White arrived at 4 PM and prepared to execute a stagecoach robbery unparalleled in the history of the Old West. From the contents of his bundle he fashioned several hoods from pieces of cloth about a foot square with holes in the opposite corners from which a cord was attached. He then dragged a large branch of wood to the center of the road and draped a large piece of canvas over it. By the roadside he laid another piece of canvas over a tree limb, thus forming a blockade for checking the stage horses. After placing a reflector light mounted on a tripod in front of the canvas by the roadside, White arranged several small tree branches around the canvas to give the impression of rifles being held by additional bandits. Settling back, he calmly awaited the arrival of the stage from Del Norte to Alamosa.[9]

Just past midnight stage driver James Downard reached the spot where White waited and was startled by a command to halt. On sighting a bandit pointing a six-shooter at him, Downard immediately stopped and exclaimed, "For God's sake, don't shoot!"

From behind the canvas by the side of the road White ordered Downard to drive forward a few feet. He then turned the reflector light so it would shine inside the stage, thus blinding the driver and passengers and rendering them incapable of knowing what was transpiring.

Ordering the driver and four passengers on top to come down, White placed hoods over their heads and commanded the other nine passengers to get out on the left side of the stage. As the bandit pointed his revolver toward the canvas, he warned them they would be shot by the men concealed behind it if they attempted anything foolish. After covering the heads of the remaining passengers until the hoods ran out, White told the rest to tie handkerchiefs over their eyes.[10]

This report in *The Denver Republican* clearly demonstrates White's classic style of stage robbery:

> When all the travelers had been thus blindfolded, their hands being then still uplifted, the bandit chief surprised them by ordering them to put their hands behind them. This maneuver quite got the better of one of the passengers, who, to save his gold watch, had put it carefully in his sleeve, where it was safe enough until the order came to put hands down, when the watch fell out into the passengers hand.
>
> "Thought to save your watch, eh?," said the bandit.
>
> "Yes," said the passenger. "It is a gift from my father now dead."
>
> "Put it in your pocket, you may keep it," was the reply.
>
> The travelers' hands were then tied behind them, after which, with hands tied and faces covered, all were searched. The bandits took no jewelry, but confined themselves almost entirely to the ready cash.
>
> "Leave me fifty cents for a drink at Alamosa," pleaded one of the victims. With grim humor the bandit put back $2.50 into the man's pocket.
>
> Having secured the money the bandit asked: "Are there any more inside the stage?"
>
> "Yes, a lady," was the reply.

"We don't rob ladies," returned the robber curtly.

Equally chivalrous was the treatment accorded a one-armed passenger. He begged not to be robbed, as he was a cripple. "We don't rob cripples," said the robber and passed on.

But less fortunate was a poor fellow who had been working in the San Juan until he had just raised money to go to Kansas to see his kindred. He was robbed of all he had, $145, and instead of visiting his friends he was compelled to work at Alamosa.

The passengers having been searched, the bandit ordered them to kneel down. He then examined the interior of the stage, and after that took charge of the mail on the coach. He compelled the lady to step out and hold a candle for him, while he opened the letters.[11]

According to newspaper reports, between eight and nine hundred dollars was taken from passengers and one thousand dollars from the mail.

Warning the passengers to be quiet while he went to the other side of the stage to see what was there, White called out to his nonexistent companions to make sure no one made a break. After fifteen minutes the woman, a Mrs. Baker from Emporia, Kansas, remarked that she thought the bandits had gone. The passengers got off their knees and found to their chagrin that Mrs. Baker was right.[12]

CHAPTER FOUR

He is the Most Incorrigible Criminal We Have Ever Seen

White arrived at Alamosa at 2 AM, preceding the stage by fifteen minutes. Returning the horse to the livery stable, he retrieved his deposit before catching the early morning train to Pueblo. The liveryman Johnson reported later that White no longer had the bundle he was carrying earlier.

A few moments after boarding the train the startled bandit nearly jumped out of his seat on catching sight of several of his robbery victims entering the car. Seating themselves at the same table with White, they began discussing the robbery without the least suspicion that among their midst sat the object of their conversation. Relaxing completely and obviously suppressing a smile, he quietly listened as they bravely related to those around them various trumped-up stories such as how they stood off the robber by refusing to get off the stage or how they hid themselves and their valuables under the seats. White later related that the passengers were very compliant and obedient and gave him no trouble whatsoever.[1]

United States Deputy Marshal M.W. Blain was in Alamosa at the time of the robbery and after receiving the news, began making inquiries in the area. Learning that a stranger had caught the morning train after returning a horse to the livery stable, Blain wired Pueblo's City Marhsal Pat Desmond to be on the lookout for the suspected bandit.

At 2 PM White stepped off the train at the Union Depot only to be arrested by Marshal Desmond. Searching his prisoner, Desmond found a total of $478, a small bag of ore and a silver watch which would later prove to be important incriminating evidence. With his suspicions satisfied the marshal marched White off to jail.

Receiving information of the arrest, an officer from Arkansas came to the jail and identified White as H.W. Burton, the robber of the Fayetteville-Alma stages. Marshal Desmond immediately sent the following telegram to U.S. Postal Inspector Carpenter in Denver:

> South Pueblo, June 29 — I have Burton, the Arkansas stage robber. He robbed the Alamosa stage night before last. What shall I do with him? P.J. Desmond, City Marshal.

Quickly wiring an answer, Carpenter requested that Desmond bring White to Denver at once.[2]

At noon on July 1 Desmond boarded the train for Denver with his prisoner. While aboard the train White vainly tried to bribe the marshal with a cock-and-bull story: offering him five hundred dollars to allow him to escape so that he could return to his home in West Virginia to hire counsel, promising he would come back to Colorado and face trial.

South of Castle Rock at a downgrade, the train reached a speed of twenty-five miles an hour. At that point Desmond left his prisoner to get a drink of water. Seeing an opportunity for escape, White stealthily left his seat and made his way to the exit. Turning around and spotting his prisoner's escape attempt, the marshal quickly rushed after him and managed to grab his coat before he could jump. Slipping out of the marshal's grasp, White leaped from the train, striking his shoulder on a railroad tie. A quick thinking passenger pulled the emergency cord while the marshal fired an ineffective shot at the fleeing bandit. After a few hundred yards the train finally stopped.

White quickly recovered from the effects of his fall and fled across country. He was seven hundred yards away by the time the train stopped and Desmond had started in pursuit. As White was lame the marshal began to close the gap. Reaching shooting range, the marshal fired several shots and brought the fugitive down with a well-placed slug that grazed the left side of his head. On reaching the fallen man the marshal was astonished to find that the fugitive had also stolen his satchel. White explained to Desmond that he took the satchel thinking there was a gun in it and then sadly remarked that he wished the marshal had killed him.[3]

U.S. Marshal P.P. Wilcox, Deputy U.S. Marshal Sim Cantril, Deputy Postal Inspector Carpenter and several county officers met the train at the Denver depot. News had leaked of White's arrival and an immense crowd had gathered at the depot to view the notorious stagecoach robber.

The officers wasted no time in bringing White before U.S. Commissioner Brazee the same day. He was remanded to the Arapahoe County jail pending a preliminary examination to be held July 8. On arrival at the jail the officers, fearing another escape attempt, took White's shoes and surprisingly found an additional fifteen dollars hidden inside.

Enough evidence was presented during the preliminary examination to have White, as Henry W. Burton, bound over for trial in the September session of U.S. District Court at Del Norte. Unable to raise the three thousand dollars bond, he remained in the Arapahoe County jail to await transfer for trial.[4]

Another Colorado stage robber named Charley Allison was in the county jail at the time that White was locked up.[5] The newspapers, having a field day at Allison's expense, now switched their attention to White.

In the ensuing months White was front page news in the Denver newspapers, with major headlines reading:

The Denver Tribune

July 1 — "Beats Billy the Kid"
July 2 — "A Cripple Highwayman"
September 25 — "The King of the Highwaymen"

The Daily News

July 7 — "Burton's Nerve"
July 9 — "Burton's Bad Dreams"
July 29 — "The Lone Hand"
August 14 — "Two Great Rogues"

The Denver Republican

July 1 — "The Drop on Burton"
July 2 — "A Dare Devil Deed"
July 9 — "Burton the Bold"

One of the first to interview White was a correspondent from *The Denver Tribune*. Reluctant to speak to the reporter, the cautious bandit avoided a long conversation by "simply stating that he was 27 years old, was a native of West Virginia, and that he had been on a trip through Colorado."

When asked by the reporter about the purpose of his trip, White answered, "My object was to buy some ranches for myself and Eastern parties."

Digging deeper, the reporter asked White how much money he had at the time of his arrest. White replied, "I had $570 and a few articles of value, but this had nothing to do with the robbery. I did not see the stage that night."

To this the correspondent retorted, "But you have a diary which shows that you were at Fayetteville, Arkansas on the 14th of June and were accused there of robbing a stage."

"It is only an unfortunate coincidence," the bandit lamely countered.

When interviewed by a correspondent from *The Denver Republican*, the wary bandit continued to evade incriminating answers, repeating what little he had told the *Tribune* reporter.[6]

White's problems mounted on July 15 when Inspector Carpenter received a package from Marshal Desmond containing the silver watch found on him after his arrest in Pueblo. This evidence coupled with a letter previously sent by H.D. Gray describing his watch in detail was enough to connect White with the Arkansas stage robberies, erasing any doubts of his guilt.[7]

To keep up public interest when no new information was forthcoming, the newspapers added their own sardonic remarks. On the death of Billy the Kid, *The Daily News* quipped: "Allison and Burton sympathize with the bereaved family and relatives of Billy, the Kid." This one-liner soon followed in the same newspaper: "Frank James is probably coming to Denver to release Allison and Burton and organize a new gang."[8]

On July 28 headline news broke when the Postal Inspectors Office released a report, based on descriptive information and a photo received from Texas, that Burton was in reality the infamous Texas bandit, Ham White. Upon receiving this information from Inspector Carpenter, *The Daily News* broke the story under the title of "The Lone Hand." Much of White's early history was reported in the article which included the incident that led to his lameness. Interviewed again by a *Daily News* reporter on the twenty-ninth, the prisoner admitted that he was Ham White and stated that the story of his career was accurately reported by the newspaper.[9]

On August 13 Inspector Carpenter questioned both White and Charley Allison in the Arapahoe County jail but neither outlaw would admit to robbing the U.S. mail. However, the session with Inspector

Carpenter shook White's confidence and caused him to have second thoughts about his previous statements to the newspapers. *The Daily News* pointed out the results:

> With reference to Burton, he refused pointblank to make any confession, or even a statement. He asserted that he never made a confession and did not expect to make one now. He denied very emphatically having uttered any of the words which appeared in a purported interview with him some weeks since, and pronounced the matter entirely and unequivocally false. [Interviews of July 29 and 30 in *The Daily News*]

> Colonel Carpenter cooly informed him that unless he made confession he would be immediately ordered back to the scenes of his misdoings where he stood a good chance of being treated in the same manner similar to Billy LeRoy. [A stage robber who had been lynched by a mob in Del Norte in May] To this the intrepid highwayman made reply that he had sooner be hanged than go to state prison for life.[10]

The Denver Tribune added:

> At that time, Burton refused to confess, and denied all knowledge of any robbery, but at the same time told Colonel Carpenter that if he could be assured that the judge would not send him up for life, he would talk with him. Of course, Colonel Carpenter could say but one thing, and that was that no man could speak for the court, but he said:

> "You might get what Billy LeRoy did and that was only ten years."

> Burton said: "If I was sure of that I might talk."[11]

White's trial was originally scheduled to commence on September 5, 1881 in U.S. District Court at Del Norte. Carpenter's threats came to naught for White was never taken to Del Norte. Rumors of the bandit's subsequent lynching led the court system to transfer his trial to U.S. District Court in Pueblo. Trial date was re-scheduled for September 21 and on September 20 the officers delivered him to the jail at Pueblo without incident.

The trial of White, as Henry W. Burton, lasted two days. With Judge Moses Hallett presiding, his trial began without benefit of an examination by a grand jury. White pled not guilty, but on the twenty-second the jury under foreman Beaufort Carpenter found him guilty of robbing the U.S. Mail and putting the life of the carrier in jeopardy. On the twenty-third Judge Hallett sentenced him to a life term at hard labor at the Wyoming Territorial Penitentiary at Laramie. On the same day an appeal and a motion for a new trial was presented by White's attorneys, Murray and Spencer, which Judge Hallett immediately denied.[12]

White realized he was in desperate straits. Figuring his chances of beating another life sentence were extremely remote he planned another escape attempt. The next day, September 24, the convicted bandit executed his plan during his transfer from Pueblo to Denver.

Upon release from his cell by the jailor, White walked into the office where U.S. Deputy Marshal Sim Cantril waited to put him in shackles. Within two feet of the marshal, he drew a fake pistol, aimed it at the marshal's heart, and ordered him to throw up his hands. The wiley bandit had made the .45 calibre replica from leather he had taken from the Denver jail, covering it with foil. As he grabbed for the marshal's pistol, Cantril jumped back and raised the shackles, intending to beat White over the head with them. Realizing his charade was over, White immediately jumped backward which, according to *The San Juan Herald*, ". . . probably saved his life, as Cantril no doubt would have broken his skull with the blow." After shackling his prisoner, Cantril delivered him to the Arapahoe County jail in Denver with no further problems.[13]

White's rash and reckless actions caused him more trouble than he bargained for. In Denver on September 28 the following telegram was sent from U.S. Marshal P.P. Wilcox to Attorney General Wayne McVeagh in Washington, D.C.:

> On twenty-second inst. H.W. Burton was convicted of mail robbery near Alamosa Col June twenty-eighth he was sentenced for life. This being his second life sentence he is now under indictment for murder in Texas he is the most incorrigible criminal we have ever seen he made one escape hereby jumping from railway train in rapid motion but was recaptured he threatens to kill the Marshal at first opportunity. The Penitentiary at Laramie City Wyoming is on border of civilization without sufficient wall around it and is wholly unsafe for such criminals we have no doubt he will escape in brief time if sent there and recommend his incarceration at Jefferson City or some other safe prison east.

The matter was presented to Judge Moses Hallett who refused to resentence White on the grounds that authorization to order a prison change must come from the U.S. Attorney General's office. On October 2 Marshal Wilcox telegraphed this information to the Attorney General and requested a change from the Wyoming Penitentiary to the House of Corrections in Detroit, Michigan.[14]

District Court.—Subpœna for Witness.—Chieftain Print, Pueblo.

UNITED STATES OF AMERICA, } ss.
District of Colorado,

The President of the United States of America,

To *L. Cass Carpenter* (Denver)

.... Greeting :

You are hereby commanded that, laying aside all business and excuses, you (and each of you,) be and appear in your proper persons before the District Court of the United States for the District of Colorado, to be held before the Judge of the said Court, at Pueblo, in the said district on the ....31st.......... *day of* ....September........ *, A. D. 1881, at* ten *o'clock in the* fore *noon, of the same day to testify all and singular those things which you know in a a certain cause now depending and undetermined in the said District Court, wherein* (the) United States of America

is plaintiff, and F. W. Burton ,

.... 10 .... *defendant,*

on the part of the Plaintiff *, and this you shall by no means omit, under the penalties imposed upon you, (and each of you,) by the law.*

Witness the Honorable Moses Hallett, Judge of the said District Court, at Pueblo, in said district, this 1st *day of* September *A. D. 1881.*

Edward F. Bishop .... Clerk.

By Wm. G. Bradford .... Deputy.

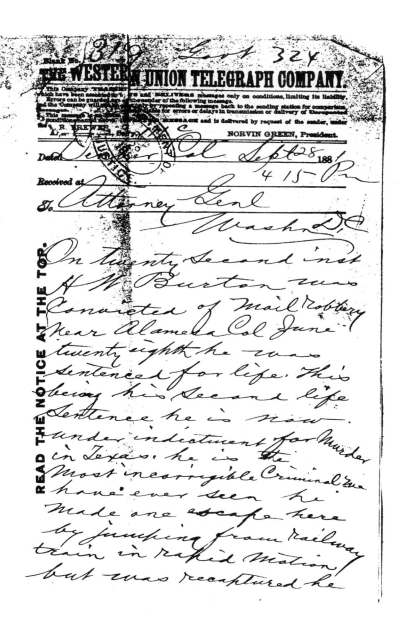

Blank No. 319 Got 324

THE WESTERN UNION TELEGRAPH COMPANY.

This Company TRANSMITS and DELIVERS messages only on conditions, limiting its liability, which have been assented to by the sender of the following message.
Errors can be guarded against only by repeating a message back to the sending station for comparison, and the Company will not hold itself liable for errors or delays in transmission or delivery of Unrepeated Messages, beyond the amount of tolls paid thereon, nor in any case where the claim is not presented in writing within sixty days after sending the message.
This is an UNREPEATED MESSAGE and is delivered by request of the sender, under the conditions named above.

A. R. BREWER, Sec'y.   NORVIN GREEN, President.

Dated _____ Cal ___ Sept 28 188__

4 15 Pm

Received at _____

To Attorney Genl

Washn D.C

On twenty second inst
H W Burton was
Convicted of mail robbery
near Alameda Cal June
twenty eighth he was
sentenced for life. This
being his Second life
Sentence he is now
under indictment for Murder
in Texas. he is the
most incorrigible Criminal we
have ever seen he
made one escape here
by jumping from railway
train in rapid motion,
but was recaptured he

THE WESTERN UNION TELEGRAPH COMPANY.

This Company TRANSMITS and DELIVERS messages only on conditions, limiting its liability, which have been assented to by the sender of the following message.
Errors can be guarded against only by repeating a message back to the sending station for comparison, and the Company will not hold itself liable for errors or delays in transmission or delivery of Unrepeated messages.
This message is an UNREPEATED MESSAGE and is delivered by request of the sender, under conditions named above.

A. R. BREWER, Secy.   NORVIN GREEN, President.

Dated _____ Sept _____ 188 /

Received at _____

To _____

threatens to kill the
Marshall at first opportunity.
The Penitentiary at Laramie City
Wyoming is on border
of Civilization without Sufficient
Wall around it &
is wholly unsafe for
Such Criminals we have
no doubt he will
escape in brief time
if Sent there &
recommend his incarceration
at Jefferson City or Some
other Safe prison east
answer.

                          P. P. Wilcox
134 paid GR   U.S. Marshall
  Br J   R. A. Cameron, Inskee
                              Post office

On October 11 the U.S. Attorney General ordered White's transfer to Detroit on the grounds that the penitentiary at Laramie was not a secure place for confinement. From Washington, acting Attorney General S.F. Phillips sent the following authorization to Wilcox on November 30:

> Authority to remove Henry W. Burton to Detroit House of Corrections was sent, as requested in your letter of October 2nd, to you in care of the Warden of the House of Correction. Remove prisoner as soon as possible.[15]

With White secured in handcuffs and leg irons, Marshal Wilcox boarded the train in Denver on December 1 and headed for Detroit. White's situation, as he saw it, was completely unfair and unjustifiable. He considered his previous escape attempts and actions acceptable: normal responses due to his circumstances. Holding Wilcox responsible and accountable for his plight, White vented his pent-up fury on the officer. This was the only premeditated act of violence on a law officer he was known to commit.

On the afternoon of December 3, while aboard the Michigan Central's day express from Chicago to Detroit, White made his move for revenge and freedom three miles east of Pokagon, Michigan. Watching out of the corner of his eye, White carefully picked the lock to his handcuffs with a toothpick while Marshal Wilcox was absorbed in reading a newspaper. Catching the marshal completely off guard, the prisoner jumped from his seat and began furiously attacking him. Beating Wilcox about the head, face, and shoulders with the handcuffs, he rendered the officer senseless. Wrenching Wilcox's revolver away from him, White unsuccessfully attempted to fire it. Fortunately for Wilcox it failed to discharge.

Along with the marshal and his prisoner, there were seventeen men and one woman aboard the railroad car. During the attack on Wilcox they all fled from the car except the plucky woman, Mrs. Alice Smithson, wife of a Denver engineer. Coming from behind and throwing her arms around White's neck she doggedly held on to the startled outlaw. While White was dancing around in the aisle with the determined woman clinging to his neck, one of the passengers alerted two guards in the baggage car. Rushing into the car the guards quickly subdued the beleaguered bandit, relieving him of his tenacious female burden.[16]

Although Wilcox sustained some hearing loss and was bruised and

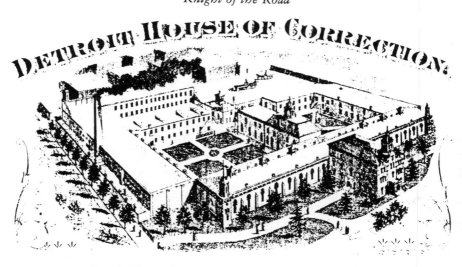

Detroit House of Correction in 1881. Authors collection.

battered, he regained his faculties and delivered White safely to the penitentiary that night. In this report in *The San Marcos Free Press*, quoted from *the New York Sun*, Wilcox, rather than expressing feelings of resentment because of the attack, gave a somewhat creditable portrayal of his assailant:

> White says if he could have got a bullet through Wilcox, he would have covered the passengers with the revolver in one hand while he untied his ankles with the other, "and then gone through every one of the infernal cowards." The Marshal says that Mrs. Smithson declined a reward, but that he is going to send to her New York address a draft of $500 before he is forty-eight hours older. . . . White is 29 years old [*sic*], of rather pleasing appearance and of gentlemanly address when he pleases. The Marshal says that he never uses profane language, and neither drinks whiskey or chews tobacco.[17]

A little over six months later White gave a much different and exaggerated version of the affair to *The Philadelphia Press*, which was quoted by *The San Marcos Free Press*:

> I was being taken from Chicago to Detroit when I disarmed the sheriff and his two deputies who had me in custody. This was in the cars. I had the sheriff's revolver pointed at his head. In an instant more I would have blown his brains out, but a passenger, Miss Alice Smith [*sic*], a lady whom I had never seen before, and whom I have never met since, threw

herself upon me, begging for the sheriff's life. I think I am too tender-hearted. Escape was open for me, but Miss Smith called out, "Think of the man's wife and children." Without a word I handed the revolver back to the sheriff, and submitted without any sound of complaint to having shackles placed upon my hands and feet.[18]

White entered the Detroit House of Corrections on December 3, 1881 under the alias of Henry W. Burton. However, his rash actions on the train caused him more trouble from the United States Justice Department. The Attorney General's Office received a report from the general agent for the Department of Justice stating that the Detroit House of Corrections did not have the proper facilities for safekeeping a dangerous criminal such as White. On May 24, 1882 Attorney General Benjamin Harris Brewster acted on this information and ordered White to be transferred from Detroit.

Upon White's discharge on May 31, U.S. Marshal S.S. Mathews of the East District of Michigan took him into custody with orders to deliver him to the Penitentiary at Philadelphia, Pennsylvania. This action would bring about more problems, however, this time White could not be held accountable. In the following telegram to the Attorney General in Washington, D.C. on June 2, Mathews demonstrated his frustration in Philadelphia:

> Warden here declines to receive Hamilton White alias Burton transferred from Detroit House of Corrections by your instructions of twenty-fourth the inspectors of the penitentiary say they can receive no one from beyond the Jurisdiction of the district court of this district. I have placed the prisoner in the station house awaiting further instructions would it not be well to instruct the Marshal of this district to relieve me and take White in charge.[19]

Quick action on the part of Attorney General Brewster solved the dilemma. On the same day, June 2, he issued the following order to the warden at the Albany County Penitentiary at Albany, New York:

> It has been represented to me by the General Agent of this Department that the present place of confinement of the said Hamilton White alias Henry W. Burton, has not the proper facilities for the safekeeping of so desperate a criminal without endangering his health, I now therefore in pursuance of the authority vested in me, by section 5546, "Revised statutes of the United States" order that the United States Marshal for the Eastern District of Michigan, proceed to the Detroit House of Correc-

tions, procure the said Hamilton White, and deliver him together with his original warrant of commitment to the Albany County Penitentiary at Albany, New York and that the said prisoner there undergo imprisonment for the balance of the term of his sentence.

Relieved at finally receiving instructions, Marshal Mathews secured his prisoner and boarded the train for Albany.

Prior to their arrival, the news that a U.S. Marshal was bringing a noted western desperado to Albany spread rapidly through the city. During this period of time the popularity of the dime novel was sweeping the eastern states. Excited with the prospect of viewing an actual celebrated highwayman who could have stepped from the pages of one of these thrillers, a huge crowd had gathered at the depot. Stepping off the train at 9:05 on the evening of June 3, the marshal and White were astonished by the crowd. Uneasy with the situation, Mathews quickly maneuvered his prisoner through the throng of people to an awaiting carriage and hurriedly delivered him to the penitentiary. Received and recorded under the alias of Henry W. Burton, Ham White began work in the prison shoe shop on the next day.[20]

CHAPTER FIVE

He is Considered one of the Most Daring Highwaymen in America

Ham White had no inten-
tion of serving out a life
sentence. He had decided that
there was no way of escape and astutely turned to the legal system to
gain his freedom. Suspecting the court had erred in their proceedings,
he retained the services of Attorney James W. Eaton, Jr. To White's
relief the records revealed that several blatant errors had been made
during his trial in Pueblo.

On January 20, 1887, by application of counsel, White appeared
before Judge Albert C. Coxe in United States District Court at Albany
on a writ of habeas corpus. The evidence was conclusive: White had not
been indicted by a grand jury; he had been tried under the name of
Burton and not his true name and therefore the court which sentenced
him did not have proper jurisdiction. Judge Coxe took little time in
concurring with the evidence and ordered White discharged from the
penitentiary the same day.[1]

After serving a little over five years of his life sentence White again
gained his freedom by using the legal system. No doubt this gratified
the crafty rogue but it did not hold the same connotations as did his
1881 release. Being freed on a technicality was not the same as a Presidential pardon and he definitely did not have the support of the majority of the citizens of Bastrop County. Due to his 1881 escapades the
stigma of "outlaw" was now and forever attached to his name.

Ironically, White would never know that on November 2, 1883 the
State of Texas dismissed the Rowe murder charge against him. Aware
that he had been convicted in a U.S. Court and was serving a life sentence, the State of Texas dropped their case.[2]

Even if White had known he was no longer wanted for murder it
was immaterial, for whatever he did from now on was academic. With

𝕿𝖍𝖊 𝕻𝖗𝖊𝖘𝖎𝖉𝖊𝖓𝖙 𝖔𝖋 𝖙𝖍𝖊 𝖀𝖓𝖎𝖙𝖊𝖉 𝕾𝖙𝖆𝖙𝖊𝖘 𝖔𝖋 𝕬𝖒𝖊𝖗𝖎𝖈𝖆

To John McOwen, Superintendant of the Penitentiary at Albany, New York.

Greeting:

You are hereby commanded that you have the body of *Camilla White (otherwise Thomas Henry Burton)* by you imprisoned and detained, as it is said, together with the time and cause of such imprisonment and detention, by whatsoever name the said *Camilla White (or Henry W. Burton)* shall be called or charged, before the Honorable *Alfred C. Coxe* Judge of the District Court of the United States for the Northern District of New York, at the United States Court Room, on the corner of *Broadway* and *State* Streets, in the City of *Albany* on the *20th* day of *January* 1889, at *10* o'clock in the *fore* noon, to do and receive what shall then and there be considered, concerning the said *Camilla White (or Henry W. Burton)* and have you then and there this writ.

WITNESS the Honorable *Alfred C. Coxe,* Judge of the District Court of the United States, for the Northern District of New York, at the City of *Albany N.Y.* the *19th* day of *January* 18*89*.

James W. Eaton Jr. Attorney.

Charles B. Germain Clerk.

58

his reputation gone, his family humiliated, and a chosen lifestyle he would not abandon, the thirty-two-year-old outlaw found himself completely alone for the first time in his life. But, being antisocial by nature, he likely found relief in being free of living up to the expectations of others.

Conditions in White's family had drastically changed since he left Bastrop County in 1881. White's mother Tabitha, who was now elderly, demented, and unable to recognize any of her children, was under the care of Ham's brother John and his wife Josie Dyer White. She was described as being "not quite right in the head," and it is probable that many family members considered her wayward son's actions contributed to her condition.[3] Whether White was aware of his mother's state of health or not, he could not return to Bastrop County believing that a murder charge was still hanging over his head. It would be many years before he would visit his homeplace again.

While learning the trade of shoemaking during his imprisonment, White obtained the locations of different shoe factories on the east coast. Upon his release he proceeded to Lynn, Massachusetts where he found work in various shoe factories.[4] No doubt life in the industrial east was bewildering to a bandit who preferred the wide-open spaces of Texas where stagecoaches were still easy prey. In Massachusetts, however, stagecoach robbery was nonexistent so he apparently remained in the east only long enough to earn passage money. By late July he was back in Texas plying his old trade.

Five years behind prison walls had not affected White's expertise in holding up stagecoaches. This he proved on the night of July 28, 1887 when he successfully held up two stagecoaches on the line between Austin and Fredricksburg. The driver of the stage headed for Fredricksburg, O.P. Beebee, was completely taken by surprise by the bandit on reaching a point two and a half miles west of Dripping Springs, Texas.

From horseback White called out to the driver to halt. Catching sight of a revolver barrel gleaming in the moonlight and pointed at his head, Beebee realized it would be foolhardy to proceed and immediately stopped. On the robber's command to get off the stage he reluctantly obeyed. After dismounting, White quickly bound and gagged the driver and, ignoring the two passengers on board, went through the mail but found no registered packages. At that point he shifted his attention to the approaching Austin bound stage.

As the passenger-free stage reached the scene of the holdup, driver K.W. McKinney found himself in the same predicament as Beebee. Ordering him to stop, White quickly went through the mail, taking only a registered pouch from Blanco. In his haste he completely overlooked another registered package on board. Not having robbed a stage in over six years, White apparently was nervous and went about his work in a cool and systematic manner, dispensing with his usual banter. On completion of the robbery he remounted and told the drivers they could proceed to their destinations. Without a word of farewell he wheeled his horse and rode off into the darkness.

The San Antonio Daily Express, in describing the robber's technique, pointed out that White's methods had changed little since his escapades in 1881.

> The man who committed the act appeared to have several men on either side of the road concealed in the bushes with whom he would hold a conversation while rifling the coaches. This, however, is now believed to have been a ruse to prevent the stage drivers or passengers making any resistance, and that the ambush was an imaginary one.[5]

The actual amount stolen from both stages was never reported in the newspapers; however, *The Austin Daily Statesman* did state: ". . . . it is not believed that much of a sum of money was obtained." This likely mattered little to White who was just enthralled with robbing stages again.

In order to outdistance any pursuers, White quickly left the scene of the robberies and headed for the eastern part of Caldwell County where, on August 2, he attended a camp meeting at Albade (now Lytton Springs), ten miles north of Lockhart. He was completely unaware that he had been seen and identified in Dripping Springs the day prior to the robberies. This information was passed on to Deputy U.S. Marshal Peavy who gathered up a posse of three men in Kyle, Texas and began tracking White, following him to Caldwell County. Arriving at Albade the officers discovered that he had just left the area. Although only hours behind the bandit, the lawmen somehow lost his trail and White fortuitously got away. *The Lockhart Register* astutely summed up the situation:

> His description tallies exactly with the person who robbed the two stages near Dripping Springs last week. . . . Ham White has robbed stages from the Mississippi river to the Pacific coast, and thoroughly

understands his business, and is considered one of the most daring highwaymen in America. He travels on his own hook and seldom has any assistance. . . . We could use several columns in reciting thrilling incidents of his life, and telling of his wild exploits on the public highway. He is a tall, red-headed ugly man and is slightly crippled. White is very crafty and will not be easily captured.[6]

A grand jury found a true bill of indictment against White, for robbery of the U.S. Mail, on August 10 in United States District Court at Austin. On February 13, 1888, six months after the indictment, the District Court issued a capias for his arrest and turned it over to U.S. Marshal John Rankin. On April 17 Rankin returned the capias with this report, "Executed after diligent search and inquiry. Not found in my District." On May 9 a second capias was issued and returned by Rankin on August 6 with the same results: "After diligent search and inquiry. Not found in my District." A final capias was issued on July 19, 1889 and turned over to U.S. Marshal Paul Fricke for execution. Having no more success than Rankin, Fricke returned the capias on August 5 with this comment, "The within named Deft. not found." Since White was not found and arrested, the court took no further action.[7]

Unknown to the officers, White had not left Texas but he had adopted a new alias, Henry A. Miller.[8] While the U.S. Marshals were looking for him, White headed westward to the little town of Stephenville in Erath County, Texas.

White likely picked Erath County because of its proximity to the vast and sparsely inhabited West Texas frontier. As one of the last jumping-off points into this enormous back country, this area would give him a decided advantage in eluding capture. Another determining factor was the easy access to stage routes running between the widely spaced west Texas towns.

During this period Stephenville was considered a mere stopping place, sporting a population of around eight hundred people. The editor of the local newspaper, *The Empire*, called Stephenville "a living disgrace. . . . no railroad, no telegraph, and it is said, no roads. As for bridges, there is not one in the county."

What outraged the editor seemingly appealed to White. On arriving in Stephenville, he had three places to lodge: Phillips Boarding House, the Stephenville House, and the newly built Tolliver Hotel. For recreation there was the Palace Saloon and billiard hall plus a race track near

CAPIAS.

No *1047*

United States of America.

District Court of the United States, Western Dist. of Texas, at Austin Sitting.

To August ___Term, 18 *89*

The President of the United States,

To the Marshal of the *Western* District of Texas, *Greeting:*

YOU ARE HEREBY COMMANDED to arrest the body of *Ham White,*

if to be found in your district, he being charged by Bill of Indictment found against him at the *August* Term, A. D. 18 *87,* of said Court, to-wit: On the *10th* day of *August* aforesaid, to-wit: That on the *28th day of July AD 1887, in the County of Hays in the Western District of Texas, did then and there unlawfully + feloniously rob one O.P. Barber, a mail carrier, + the said Ham White in effecting said robbery did put in jeopardy the life of the said O.P. Beebe, + on said date did unlawfully + feloniously rob one K.W. McKinney, a mail carrier entrusted with the U.S. Mail, and in effecting said robbery did put in jeopardy the life of said K.W. McKinney, mail carrier as aforesaid, by the use of a pistol, then + there a dangerous weapon ___*

Contrary to the Statutes in such cases made and provided, and against the peace and dignity of the United States and him, safely keep, and have you his body before our said Court on the *1st Monday it being the 5th day of August* A. D. 188 *9,* with this writ, showing how you have executed the same *D.S. Maxey* WITNESS, the Honorable *E. B. Turner,* Judge of the District Court of the United States for the Western District of Texas, and the Seal of our said Court at Austin, this *19th* day of *July* A. D. 18 *89*

D.H. Hart, Clerk

By_____*Deputy.*

town.[9] In this ideal retreat, the wanted outlaw encountered the unexpected; for the first and only time in his life Ham White fell in love.

Although White had many vices he definitely was not the Lothario type. No newspaper or public document ever connected him with any other woman or hinted that he was romantically inclined. There is no

Printed and for sale by Clarke & Courts, Stationers, Printers, Lithographers and Blank Book Manufacturers, Galveston.

MARRIAGE RECORD.

STATE OF TEXAS, ERATH COUNTY.

To any Judge of the County or District Court, Ordained Minister of the Gospel, or Justice of the Peace, in and for said County, Greeting:

You are hereby authorized to SOLEMNIZE THE RITES OF MATRIMONY *between*

Mr. *Henry A. Miller* and *Miss Nannie C. Scott*

and make due return to the Clerk of the County Court of said County within sixty days thereafter, certifying your action under this License.

WITNESS my official signature and seal of office, at office in Stephenville, this 5th

{Seal}

day of *December* A.D. 188 7

John S. Hyatt
Clerk of the County Court, Erath County.

By *C. R. Shepherd* Deputy.

I, *O. W. Hughart*, hereby Certify that on the 7th day of *December* A.D. 188 7, I united in Marriage *Henry A. Miller* and *Miss Nannie C. Scott* the parties above named.

WITNESS my hand this 8th day of *December* A.D. 188 7

O. W. Hughart
Minister of the Gospel

Filed for Record this 15th day of *December* A.D. 188 7

John S. Hyatt County Clerk.

By *C. R. Shepherd* Deputy.

doubt that White deeply cared for this woman in Stephenville as he later expressed genuine concern for her welfare as records point out.

All that is known of the lady in question is her name, Nannie C. Scott, and that she resided in Stephenville at the time White met her. At what point in time or how the two met is unknown but after a short courtship White, as Henry A. Miller, and Miss Scott were married in Stephenville on December 7, 1887 by Reverend O.W. Hughart, Minister of the Gospel. The pair settled in a little village in the eastern portion of Erath County called Duffau, named in honor of an Indian known as Duffo who was buried nearby.[10]

If White actually intended to reform he picked a most inopportune time to do it. Economically the small farmer and rancher were being strangled. If disastrously high prices were not enough the awesome 1886 blizzard and the long droughts of 1886 – 1887 sealed their doom. Soon thousands of disillusioned men of the soil left Texas to take up tenant farming or accept low-paying, back-breaking jobs in the industrial east.[11]

The economic conditions in Texas during 1887 may have been a factor in White's return to outlawry, especially if he and Nannie Scott had already met and planned marriage. More likely it was his obsession with stage robbery since he waited only two months after the July robberies to strike again.

CHAPTER SIX

I'm a Dandy, Ain't I

In late September, 1887 Ham White unleashed his first strike in a series of stage robberies on the Ballinger and San Angelo Stage Line. Although never officially charged or indicted for these robberies, there can be no doubt of his guilt. The robbery methods, the polite treatment of the passengers, and the gallantry shown towards women were typical White trademarks. But the clincher and most damning proof of his involvement was his ever-present game right leg. More important than the robberies themselves, however, was the impact they had on the United States judicial system, not to mention personal agonies and the excessive costs to the United States government.

The holdups began at 11:30 on the night of September 29. As the stage from San Angelo reached a spot known as Nichol's pasture, ten miles outside of Ballinger, White rode up with a red handkerchief over his face and ordered driver Armon Broom to stop. There were seven passengers aboard: Ed Kaufman, Charles Duffy, O.M. Latimer, J.M. Taylor, P.D. Preston, Joseph Rass, and S.W. Titus. Commanding them to step down, White handed each one a crude bag made from an old slicker and ordered them to put them over their heads. In a leisurely manner, he relieved them of $880. One of the passengers begged the bandit to leave him enough to buy a meal. Complying, he unknowingly handed the man a twenty dollar gold piece. He discovered his error after counting the loot and took back the gold piece, giving the man a dollar in exchange.

Turning his attention to the mail, White cut the bag and removed its contents. Under the threat of his revolver, he kept the passengers standing until the stage from Ballinger arrived three hours later. While waiting for the second stage, White kept up such pleasant banter with his captives that one, S.W. Titus, actually tried to sell him a windmill.

On the arrival of the second stage, White allowed his captives to get back on their stage and leave. Stopping driver William Ellis, he conducted his second robbery in the same manner as he had the first. Politely refusing to rob the two women passengers, he took $137 dollars from the men: Reverend J.H. Zivley, Reverend J.H. Stanley, Tom Sanderson, and E. Haribut. Apparently the waiting had made White somewhat nervous as he began waving his revolver around in a reckless manner until one of the passengers asked him to be a bit more careful. He good-naturedly acknowledged the request and lowered his pistol. From the registered packages he obtained sixty-five dollars but found nothing on rifling the U.S. Mail. As a finale, the bandit mounted his horse and rode off at a full gallop, firing his revolver twice and letting out a whooping cry.

Reaching their destination, the victims of both robberies described the robber as five-foot-eight or -nine inches in height, about 135 pounds, light complexioned, wearing a dark soft hat, light-colored jeans and coat, and favoring his right leg. He rode a dark brown horse about fourteen-hands-high. When the news reached Postal Inspector Hollingsworth in Austin, he issued a reward of two hundred dollars for the bandit.[1]

Pleased with his success White threw all caution to the wind and decided to try his luck again. Finding a safe refuge, he hid out for three days. Then, on October 3, at the same time and same location, he struck the stage line again. Stopping stage driver William Ellis for the second time in three days, the stage robber handed each of the four passengers a hood made from a slicker with orders to place them over their heads. From D.P. Gay he took only three dollars but got nothing from W.H. Preston. One of the two women passengers handed White forty-five dollars but, in his usual gallant manner, he refused the money remarking that he never took money from ladies. A search through the registered mail yielded him only ten dollars.

Before departing, White told the driver not to leave until he heard a shot that would signal that he had stopped the other stage. After an unavailing wait of three hours, the driver proceeded to Ballinger. The signal never came because the outgoing stage had eluded the bandit by taking a different route. The passengers gave the same description of the robber as was given previously. As an interesting note, over a year later the press lamely tried to shift the blame to Eugene Bunch, a notorious train robber of the period.[2]

According to Preston in his testimony as a U.S. government witness, this conversation took place during the holdup:

> He asked to know what time it was. I told him 12:05. He said I will give myself half hour on the mail and then go to the other stage. I asked him what he got out of the other stage and he said over a thousand. I asked him if that wasn't a good days work. He replied yes but he was not satisfied with that. I asked him if he was going to fool around and get caught for $10 as he only got $10 out of the mail on my stage. Mr. Gay asked him if he thought he would be caught. He told him he did not think there were enough men in Concho County to take him alive. He then went off to rob the other stage the signal was to fire his gun off but he did not fire it.[3]

Unbelievably the next night White was again in the same location waiting to rob the Ballinger bound stage. *The Waco Examiner* reported what occurred, even to the point of naming White as the bandit:

That Notorious Highwayman

> Instead of running the regular mail hack last night the mail was sent over in a buggy and the passenger stage followed today. As the buggy containing the mail reached the same place the stage had been robbed so often before it was halted by the same man, but after asking several questions relating to some sheep, he was allowed by the party to go forward. The description given of this man conforms in every respect to that of the robber. A great many think he is the notorious stage robber Sam [*sic*] White, who is said to wear a vest of steel.[4]

Apparently alarmed when the newspaper identified him as the bandit, White fled the hundred or so miles to Erath County where, as Henry Miller, he could live in relative safety without the least suspicion of being the stage robber. If it meant anything at all to the bandit, his escapades had caused the stage line to initiate the unprecedented step of rerouting all the stage runs and changing the schedules entirely to the daylight hours to prevent further robberies.[5]

These three stage robberies also brought about a terrible and blatant miscarriage of justice. At eleven o'clock on Sunday night, October 9, Runnels County Sheriff John W. Formwalt and Texas Ranger John A. Brooks arrested a twenty-six-year-old cowboy, James Alfred Newsome, in Coleman, Texas for the robberies. The only evidence against him was circumstantial and inadequate: on October 7 he purchased a stock of horses from rancher Tom Landers for seven hundred dollars and had a hundred dollar bill changed at the county treasurers office. U.S. Marshal J.M. Waller brought Newsome to Waco via the Missouri Pacific Railroad on October 14 where he was confined in the McLennan County jail.

The next day at 10 AM Newsome was given an examination before U.S. Commissioner J.H. Finks for the early morning robberies of September 30. Of the three witnesses only Reverend Zivley positively identified him as the stage robber. On this evidence he was bound over on $2,500 bail to await action by the grand jury. On November 16 Newsome appeared at his second examination for the October 3 robbery. Nevertheless, on November 25 the grand jury indicted him for robbing the U.S. Mail and putting into jeopardy the life of said carrier of mail.[6]

On December 8, the day after White's marriage, Newsome came to trial for White's crimes in U.S. District Court at Waco under Judge A.P. McCormick. Of all the witnesses only Reverend Zivley remained adamant in his identification of him. Reverend Stanley stated he could not positively identify him as the bandit but thought he was the man. Witnesses S.W. Titus, W.H. Preston, and O.M. Latimer stated that Newsome, who was five feet, ten and a half inches tall, was taller than the bandit who was five feet, eight or nine inches in height. All remarked that the bandit favored his right leg which Newsome did not.

Several defense witnesses from Coleman County swore that Newsome was nowhere near the robbery scene on September 29 or October 3, and all accounted for his whereabouts on both nights. The defendant also proved that he purchased the horses on credit and obtained the hundred dollar bill legally.

Despite Newsome's strong defense, the jury found him guilty on December 9 and Judge McCormick sentenced him to life imprisonment at the Albany County Penitentiary in New York, the same prison where White had obtained his release one year earlier. On January 6, shortly after Newsome had been taken to the penitentiary, 113 citizens of Paint Rock and Concho County drew up and signed a petition testifying to his innocence.[7] It had no effect on his conviction but did show the general consensus of the people.

For the next three months all remained quiet and the matter was considered closed until April 20, 1888 when two more stages from Ballinger were robbed in broad daylight. Six months had passed since White's last robbery but the situation had changed drastically. An innocent man was in prison on his account which preyed on his mind and economically, times were hard. Since no one suspected him, he could rectify it all by robbing another stagecoach.

A grey, cool, and wet morning greeted White when he made his fourth trip to Nichol's Pasture outside of Ballinger. Wearing a slicker and concealing his face with a white handkerchief, he took the time to disguise his roan horse, covering the body with blankets and the legs with little sacks. Leaning against a mesquite tree nearby, he patiently waited for the Ballinger bound stage.

Running late, stage driver William Ellis had no thoughts of stage robbery at 10:20 that morning. He was much more concerned with the slow pace the swaying stage was forced to travel because of the muddy conditions. Anyway, the bandit had been caught and convicted.

Approaching Nichol's Pasture, Ellis was shocked at the sight of a masked man leaning against a mesquite tree with his masked horse nearby. Taking a closer look, his initial shock turned to resignation when he realized the man was armed and certainly meant business. Being victimized for the third time, Ellis knew exactly what to expect.

Pushing himself away from the tree and pointing his silver-plated Colt .45 at Ellis, White commanded him to halt. Out of the corner of his eye he spotted a six-passenger, two-horse hack following in the wake of the stage. The hack driver, Al Jacks, noticed the bandit at the same time and frantically tried to change direction. Anticipating Jacks' move, and keeping his eye on Ellis, White outmaneuvered the hack driver and stopped him cold.

With the realization that they were going to be robbed, the frenzied passengers began shoving money and valuables in various hiding places within the stage and on their persons. One man shoved twenty dollars down his shirt front while another ingenious passenger, not knowing what to do, stuffed a sixty-dollar wad of bills in his mouth where it remained during the entire ordeal. Another man panicked and threw a $175 gold watch out the window but was unable to find it after the robbery.

Gathering the ten passengers and both drivers into one long line and handing them hoods made from saddle blankets, he pleasantly asked them to put them over their heads. Discovering that he did not have enough hoods to go around, White apologized for not being able to accommodate them all and politely insisted the others blindfold themselves with their handkerchiefs.

White leisurely and methodically began taking money and valuables from his victims. San Angelo resident Eugene Cartledge, on giving up a gold watch to the bandit, told him he would hate to lose the watch as it contained hair from several of his family members and was an heirloom. Without hesitation, White returned it with a smile. Finishing with the passengers, who contributed $112, he turned to Ellis and told him to cut the mail bag from which he extracted an additional forty dollars. The situation was made more spectacular by the fact that freight wagons were periodically passing in full view of the robbery on an adjacent road.

White allowed several passngers to remove their hoods, informing them that they were all going to wait until the stage from Ballinger arrived. Mounting his horse, the bandit began conversing with his captives. After asking Ellis what had become of the smooth-faced driver [Armon Broom] he had robbed last fall, White began describing in detail incidents that occurred during his previous robberies. He ended his narrative with, "They haven't got me yet; I'm a dandy ain't I?"

Falling into this strange comradery, the passengers began bantering with him. Discovering that one of his victims, Mike J. Jacobs, was a cigar drummer, White had him pass out cigars to the entire crowd.

At this time the most noted outlaw in Texas was Rube Burrow whose gang had committed their second train hold-up at Benbrook, Texas the previous September and had recently robbed another at Genoa, Arkansas. The passengers, in jest, began referring to White as "Rube." Enjoying the charade and with mock severity, the stage robber asked his victims to please refer to him as Mr. Borrows [*sic*].[8] One passenger jokingly requested for "Rube" to write a statement absolving them of cowardice. Complying, White wrote the following on a drummers card from the pommel of his saddle:

THE FOLLOWING CERTIFICATE:

This is to certify that I believe you gentlemen would have made a fight if you had been armed. This is to clear you before the public of cowardice.

Rube Borrows [*sic*][9]

When questioned about his chances of successfully escaping, White remarked that if caught he expected to be taken dead and that on his person were papers that would completely absolve Jim Newsome of any guilt. Becoming more familiar, one passenger asked him why he did not rob trains which were much more profitable. He readily replied that accomplices were necessary to rob a train and one of them might squeal on him. Continuing his explanation, the congenial bandit remarked that he preferred this special line of business as he could accomplish it single-handedly. In an offhand and satirical manner, White added that he was not afraid of the ranger who only went out in good weather.

Patiently waiting until 3 PM for the incoming stage which had been delayed because of the muddy roads, White allowed his victims to leave, warning them that if they encountered the stage, to let it pass as if nothing had occurred; otherwise, he threatened, something would happen. Accompanying the stage as far as Willow Water Hole Station, he gave each passenger enough money for a meal before bidding them farewell and departing. Fortunately for White, he was long gone when the two stages met a short time later as the incoming stage contained a Deputy Sheriff and another officer, both of whom were armed.

Reaching San Angelo at 8 PM, the passengers and Ellis related that the robber's face was completely covered with a handkerchief, except for his grey-green eyes, and he was wearing brogan shoes. They stated that he spoke very fluently in a soft voice and used no slang. Everyone agreed there was no doubt that he was the bandit who robbed the stages the previous fall.

The Galveston Daily News, after interviewing Ellis, stated in their April 22 issue:

> Mr. Ellis, the stage driver, who also drove one of the stages that was robbed last fall, says that, judging from his stature, pistol and voice, he feels confident that he is the same man.

On the morning of the twenty-first the sheriff and three rangers left Ballinger in pursuit of the bandit, hoping to follow his tracks. By that time, however, White was well on his way back to Erath County.[10]

Regarding White's action during the robbery, *The San Angelo Standard* quipped: "That Ballinger and San Angelo stage robber missed his vocation. He should be editing a humorous paper."[11]

Since James Newsome's conviction in December, his attorneys, Andrews and Lessing, had been hard at work in his behalf. On December 10, 1887 the attorneys made a motion for a new trial which was refused. According to law they could not appeal a conviction handed down in a U.S. Court, so they filed a petition for writ of error to Circuit Judge Don A. Pardee in Dallas. The petition was still pending when the latest stage robbery occurred; now the attorneys had something concrete with which to work. On April 26 Attorney William H. Lessing wrote an article which was published in the *San Angelo Standard* outlining these new developments.[12]

The situation remained unchanged until June 23 when the stage from San Angelo was robbed again. At 3:00 PM, three miles east of Willow Water Hole Station, driver Al Jacks noticed a man about 150 yards ahead walking leisurely towards San Angelo. As the stage approached, the man pulled a blue handkerchief over his face. The passengers, thinking he was trying to keep the sun off his face, began joking with him to hold up. Taking their advice, White pulled a revolver and told the driver to "hold up."

As in his previous robberies, White made the seven passengers step down, put handkerchiefs over their faces, and relieved them of $260. He promptly returned a gold watch to passenger Harry Bennett after being told it belonged to someone else. For some reason he did not bother with the registered mail. Finding a whiskey flask in Bennett's valise, the generous bandit set up drinks for the entire crowd. Improvising his technique, White then had the driver remove the near-wheel horse which he mounted bareback and rode off towards Sweetwater.

As soon as the stage reached Ballinger, Sheriff Formwalt set out with bloodhounds after the highwayman. Meanwhile, passenger Harry Bennett of the Legal Tender Saloon in San Angelo identified the robber as John Gray, gambler and stockman from Nolan County. Gray, known as Long John, had arrived in San Angelo three weeks previously. A few nights before the robbery, while in the Legal Tender Saloon, he borrowed a revolver from another gambler named John Brown. On receipt of this information, Sheriff Dick Ware of Mitchell County arrested him at Colorado City on June 28. From there Gray was transferred to the jail at San Angelo.

On July 11 U.S. Deputy Marshal J.H. Bull arrived in San Angelo with a bench warrant for Gray. Receiving the prisoner from Sheriff

Willis Johnson, the marshal took him to Waco by stage the next day and locked him up in the McLennan County jail.[13]

Gray, as innocent as Newsome, was determined to avoid trial for a crime he did not commit. At 3:00 on October 8 he made a desperate bid for freedom. As Deputy Sheriff Sam Whatley, who was bringing dinner to the prisoners, stepped into the corridor, Gray grabbed him around the waist while another prisoner choked him into unconsciousness. Gray snatched up the keys and quickly liberated five other prisoners. Locking up the turnkey and obtaining two revolvers, the escapees made a dash for the street.

Two of the escaped prisoners, Bob and Don Campbell, overpowered a constable and took his horse. Mounted double, the Campbells led the rest of the escapees across a bridge over the Brazos River to the railroad tracks. Gray and the Campbells stole a Missouri Pacific handcar and headed north until they met an oncoming train which forced them to abandon it. The sheriff and local police wasted no time; with the help of several citizens they had all the escapees recaptured within three hours. Returning to the McLennan County jail, one of the escapees drolly remarked to a newspaper reporter, "We just done this to give you fellows an item."[14]

On October 20 Gray appeared before U.S. Commissioner Finks for a preliminary examination on the charge of delaying the U.S. mail and putting the life of the driver in jeopardy. After four witnesses presented evidence, Commissioner Finks set his bail at two thousand dollars for each case. Unable to raise bail, he was remanded to the McLennan County jail to await action by the grand jury.[15]

News of the robbery and Gray's arrest benefited Jim Newsome's case. On June 30 Associate Justice of the U.S. Supreme Court Lucius Quintus Cincinnatus Lamar officially notified his attorneys that, upon receiving a two hundred dollar bond, he would at once grant the petitioner a writ of error. The attorneys complied and on August 7 the writ was allowed. On December 10 the U.S. Circuit Court at Waco handed down an order allowing the writ of error to be argued before Associate Justice Lamar at such time and place as may suit the convenience of the Circuit Justice and by agreement of all parties.

Another six months passed before further action was taken. On June 8, 1889 Attorney Lessing appeared alone in Newsome's defense before Justice Lamar in U.S. Circuit Court in Dallas. On Lessing's evidence, Justice Lamar reversed the verdict of the U.S. District Court at Waco and ordered a new trial for Newsome. According to *The Waco Daily News*, this decision set a precedent in U.S. law: it was the first conviction in a U.S. Court in Texas that had ever been reversed.[16]

This was not the only setback the U.S. District Court at Waco was to suffer. Taking into account the reversal of the court's decision in Newsome's trial, the United States took a long look at the case they had against Gray. It was evident that they had the wrong man again and, on April 16, 1889, a writ was granted on grounds that the government could offer no proof against Gray and he was officially discharged.[17]

In July, 1889, after serving eighteen months in prison, James Newsome was released from the Albany County Penitentiary and brought to Waco. On July 29, pending trial, he was granted bail in the amount of five thousand dollars. Ironically, one of his bondsmen, D.P. Gay, had been a victim of the October 3 robbery. Newsome's case, scheduled to be tried in U.S. District Court in Waco on November 21, was continued on the grounds that several material witnesses failed to appear.

For over a year Newsome remained free on bond until his case came up for trial on December 12, 1890. All the witnesses for the prosecution claimed that he was not the stage robber except Reverend Zivley, who continued to insist that he was guilty.[18] The case ended the next day with predictable results. The headlines and excerpts from *The Waco Daily News* gave the best summation:

HE IS FREE AT LAST

James Newsome, Who Got a Life Time, Out.

The result is known. The cause was reversed and the defendant was admitted to bail in the sum of $5,000 since which time he has been under bond. From this moment the case was in effect beat, and the trial Saturday was but an expression of the popular proclamation that Newsome was innocent.

Besides reporting the result of Newsome's trial, the headlines of *The Waco Daily News* also left its readers with this reminder, "The Lone Highwayman Still At Large."[19]

In the sanctuary of Erath County Ham White could relax and reflect on his success during the past year and the problems they created. Just by reading the newspapers he could see the furor his actions had caused. With this in mind, he realized that if he held up another stage in Texas and got caught, the U.S. Government, in their embarrassment, would lock him up and throw away the key.

After the marriage, just how White explained or justified his periodic absences to his wife is not known. Whatever he told her had a satisfactory effect for neither she or the residents of Erath County suspected him of the stage robberies. In time, however, White did leave his wife and the confines of Erath County to resume his lawless course.

As far as can be determined only Erath County Sheriff Nathan J. Shands offered any statement regarding White's departure. On request for information about White, as Henry Miller, Sheriff Shands wrote a letter in 1891 to U.S. Marshal George Gard in Los Angeles, California. On receipt of this information from the marshal, *The Los Angeles Times* wrote the following terse statement:

> Sheriff N.J. Shands writes the Marshal that while Miller lived at Stephenville he married a Miss Scott. After living with her for a short time he deserted her. She is still living there.[20]

Marital problems were not a factor and White certainly did not desert his wife for documented evidence proves that he later provided monetary support and kept in friendly contact with her. There is no reason to doubt White's intention to return to her. That had been his pattern in the past and there is nothing in the records to indicate otherwise.

This raises the question of why he left home. One unfortunate incident that occurred in 1888 was the death of White's mother.[21] If White was aware of her death, it would have left him with feelings of guilt and shame but certainly not wanderlust. The logical reasons behind his departure were monetary problems, restlessness and, of course, his incessant urge to rob stagecoaches. From past actions it is not hard to figure out how he would go about solving his dilemma.

For whatever reasons, White left Erath County no later than mid-November of 1888. With the realization that it would be foolhardy to commit any more crimes in Texas, he headed west for Arizona where he had heard that robbing stagecoaches was like "taking candy from a baby."

CHAPTER SEVEN

God Damn You, I'll Shoot

Ham White went to Arizona in 1888 to rob stage-coaches. A clue to what possessed him to go there can be found in the contents of a letter written by a man who would become his bitterest enemy. Although the letter was written in 1891, it is evident that the same information had been reported in various newspapers in Texas and that White read these accounts.

The author of the letter was Dr. J.M. Hurley, a San Bernadino, California physician and Arizona rancher whose hatred for outlaws would later cause White great misfortune. Hurley's letter, written to the U.S. Postmaster General in Washington, D.C., outlined the situation in southern Arizona:

> Permit me to call your attention to the often repeated robbries [*sic*] of the United States mails in Southern Arizona, and especially on the mail route from Florence to Cassa Grande [*sic*].
>
> The mail stage on this ruit [*sic*] has been robbed with impunity for years; the police of the Territory seem to be unable to suppress it, or bring the highwaymen to justice.
>
> When the Mexican highwayman swoops down upon a stage load of passengers and mail, there is a flurry in official circles for a short time, and then quietude reigns until the freebooter suddenly makes his appearance again. Rewards are all well enough in place, but here they have failed to accomplish much. In my opinion nothing short of special detectives, who are unknown to any except those who are in the confidence will succeed.
>
> I would suggest one of these located, as a settler on a Homestead on the margin of the settlement about 10 miles South-west of Florence, and

another about six miles North-east of Cassa Grande [*sic*]; this will leave about 10 miles between to be especially looked after and the section where the roberies [*sic*] have always been committed.

This section is unsettled, and the Desert containing sufficient brush to enable the highwaymen to soon get out of sight.[1]

One is drawn to the similarity between the holdup White was soon to commit and those described in Hurley's letter, especially the exact location of the robbery site. The irony and, for White, the tragedy was that his primary victim was Dr. J.M. Hurley.

The first record of White's appearance in Arizona occurred on November 21, 1888 when he arrived at Florence on a stage from Casa Grande, waybilled as Henry Brown. Departing at the stage office, he took his blanket roll and disappeared. The next evening he entered Sam Bostic's Barber Shop, got a shave and again disappeared.[2]

On the morning of the twenty-third White left Florence on a bay horse which he apparently obtained from a livery. Proceeding to Oneida Station about nine miles northeast of Casa Grande, he concealed himself behind some bushes and waited for the stage for Florence. Dr. J.M. Hurley and his hired man, W. Jeff LaBarron, were traveling the same road by buggy from Hurley's Arizona ranch to Casa Grande. Shortly after twelve noon, driving up to where White was hidden behind the brush, the two men were ordered to hold up.

White, wearing a mask cut from a blanket and armed with a sawed-off double-barreled shotgun, made the pair drive their buggy behind the bushes. He then threw out two gunny sack hoods with eye holes to Hurley and ordered both men to put them over their heads. Going through their pockets, he removed fifty-three dollars and a watch from Hurley. After being robbed, Hurley asked White if he could drive on to Casa Grande. The bandit curtly replied that they would have to remain until he robbed the stagecoach.

Shortly thereafter, E.A. Saxe of Casa Grande drove up in his wagon and was given the same treatment as Hurley and LaBarron, except that he was not robbed. For two hours White held the three hooded men captive while conversing with them in his usual glib manner. At one point he asked Hurley for a drink of water. Consequently, the three captives got a good look at his features when he lifted his mask to drink. The prisoners also observed that he was wearing a blanket around his hips in an attempt to hide his game leg.

Around 2 PM, as the stage from Florence drove up, White called out from behind the bushes and ordered driver George Cummins to halt. Noting the hooded men, Cummins immediately complied as he thought there were four robbers instead of one. The bandit commanded Cummins to throw out the express box and mail bags. Ripping open the four mail sacks, he removed thirteen registered letters containing twenty-eight dollars and twenty-five cents and around ten dollars from the Wells Fargo's express box. He ordered Hurley to return the scattered mail to the sacks and throw it back into the stage. After returning Hurley's watch, White released his victims and disappeared into the brush.[3]

As soon as the stage reached Casa Grande, news of the robbery was telegraphed to Under Sheriff J.D. Thomas in Florence. Thomas and J.P. Gabriel immediately left town and headed for the robbery site. By the time the two officers reached their destination a heavy rainstorm had begun, obliterating the bandit's trail. However, *The Arizona Weekly Enterprise* printed this fairly accurate description of White provided by his victims:

> The robber was about 5 feet 9 inches in height; wore black pants and vest and blue shirt, and where the mask failed to cover his neck the skin indicated a dark complexion.[4]

Throughout his lifetime White shifted from periods of cleverness and shrewdness to intervals marked by irrationality and poor judgment. White's next move demonstrates the latter case as he unaccountably followed his victims to Casa Grande. Although Casa Grande was significantly closer to the robbery site than any other fair-sized town, what would possess him to go there when the odds of being recognized were so high? Possibly his statement to the Texas rangers in 1877 would apply here: ". . . it was no use in a man tearing himself all to pieces in the brush after he had made a good haul."[5] Since no one ever bothered to ask him this question, it will forever remain unanswered.

Nevertheless, White did go to Casa Grande, arriving there the same evening of the robbery. The next day the apparently unconcerned bandit leisurely strolled through the streets of the town wearing the same clothes he had worn during the robbery. E.A. Saxe happened to be on the street at the same time and recognized him at once. Needless to say, Saxe summoned Constable D.W. Cummins who promptly arrested him without resistance. A search of White's pockets turned up thirty-five dollars in gold and silver. The officer found additional currency in the lining of his hat. The prisoner gave his name as Henry Miller and stated that he had a wife in Texas.

On the day of his capture an official complaint citing the Territory of Arizona against Henry Miller for robbery was issued in Justice Court under Justice of the Peace Charles M. Marshall. On Monday morning, November 26, all the victims positively identified White as the robber during his preliminary examination trial held under Justice Marshall. Bound over to appear before the grand jury, he waived his right to make a statement. Unable to raise the ten thousand dollar bail, he was taken into custody by officers J.P. Gabriel, A. Price, and D.W. Cummins who delivered him to the Pinal County jail at Florence the same night.[6]

On November 30, obviously hoping for leniency in his upcoming trial, White broke down and confessed to the robbery. *The Arizona Weekly Enterprise* gave the following details:

> Henry Miller, alias Henry Brown, now held in the county jail charged with the stage robbery on Friday of last week, made a full confession of guilt yesterday morning to Justice C.M. Marshall, of Casa Grande, who visited him in his cell. He says he was out of money and could find no work and he conceived the idea of robbing the stage, inspired by the success of the California and other Arizona men of that stamp. He told where his gun and the masks were concealed and Mr. Marshall intended visiting the place on his return trip to Casa Grande.[6]

If Marshall retrieved White's gun and masks it was not reported. In Florence, on December 11, the grand jury in Pinal County District Court, Second Judicial District of the Territory of Arizona, found three bills of indictment against White: Case number 20 for the robbery of Dr. Hurley, Case number 21 for the robbery of Wells Fargo's express box, and Case Number 22 for assault with the intent to commit robbery against E.A. Saxe. The prisoner was bound over for trial in the December term of District Court.

Tried as Henry Miller, White appeared before Judge W.H. Barnes on December 12 and pled guilty to the crime of robbery. Attorney G.H. Gury represented White and District Attorney W.E. Sloan handled the prosecution for the Territory of Arizona. Accepting the prisoner's plea, the court fixed December 13 as the date of sentencing. He was found guilty on only one charge, for robbing Wells Fargo's express box. On receiving White's statement that he had no legal cause to show why judgment should not be passed, Judge Barnes sentenced him to serve twelve years in the Arizona Territorial Prison at Yuma.[8]

The Arizona Weekly Enterprise reported the convicted bandit's reaction to his sentence:

> He received his sentence complaisantly and seemed unmoved when it was pronounced having evidently nerved himself for the ordeal. But as he was conducted from the courtroom to the jail he seemed to be in a dazed condition and could only mutter "twelve years — twelve years." On reaching his cell he gave way to his grief and came very near fainting. He is a quite intelligent man of perhaps 26 years of age of pleasant appearance and has not the look of a bravado or hardened criminal. He is lame in one leg and walks with a slight limp. His term of imprisonment will take the best years of his life and it is hoped that he may come forth a reformed man.[9]

Sheriff Fryer removed White from the Pinal County jail on the fourteenth and delivered him to the Territorial Prison the next day. He was registered as Henry Miller, convict number 556; nativity —Texas; Age — 35; poor education but able to read and write; occupation — laborer; height — five feet nine and a half inches; complexion — light; eyes — blue; hair — light; and date of discharge under commitment — 17, August, 1896.[10]

In addition to the letter quoted at the start of this chapter, Dr. Hurley wrote a follow-up letter to the Chief Post Office Inspector in Washington in reference to the lawless conditions in southern Arizona. In the letter, dated May 21, 1891, Hurley made this surprising revelation regarding White's case: "You refer to the case of Miller and my relations with it. Will say that it is the only case in Arizona that has been brought to justice and that was through my efforts."[11]

Shortly after White's arrest and subsequent indictments by the Territory of Arizona, the United States Post Office Department began their own investigation because U.S. mail had been stolen. On November 30, Chief Post Office Inspector S.A. Kirkwood wrote to Postmaster John Miller in Florence, Arizona requesting information on White's arrest and the details of the crime. By the time the Post Office Department had enough evidence to indict him, it was too late and the Postal authorities had no recourse but to let Territorial law take its

Arizona Territorial Penitentiary at Yuma in the 1890s.

course. The Post Office Department, however, did not intend to drop the matter.

A few days after White was incarcerated at Yuma, he was visited by U.S. Postal Inspector D.O. Herbert. According to Inspector Herbert, he obtained a paper signed by the prisoner authorizing and directing Sheriff Fryer of Pinal County to turn over the amount taken from the U.S. Mail to him. In Herbert's words:

> My recollection is that I promised Miller that the paper which he was then signing should not be used against him in future trial and should only be used for the purpose of obtaining the money from the sheriff. . . . I perhaps also said to him that the Government would be more disposed to be lenient towards him, if he showed a disposition to make restitution, and also perhaps, I thought that he had been sufficiently punished and that I would use any influence that I might have to save him from further prosecution, if he would aid me in making restitution.

This paper was subsequently sent to Sheriff Fryer who forwarded the money to Herbert who turned it over to the Post Office Department.[12]

White, on the other hand, had a somewhat different recollection regarding Herbert's visit:

> A few days after I was sent to Yuma the U.S. mail inspector came to see me and in the presence of the Deputy Warden he promised me that if I would make good the money that was stolen from the mail I should not be prosecuted. I did as he requested thinking he had the power to make good his promise.[13]

The significance of this visit, which would become a key issue later, is whether or not Herbert promised White immunity. But this was not the only controversy that confronted the U.S. Postal authorities.

Immediately following the robbery the United States Post Office offered a reward of two hundred dollars for the arrest and conviction of the U.S. mail robber. On November 30, 1888 Justice of the Peace Marshall filed a claim for the reward. Post Office Inspector Herbert had been assigned to the case and duly turned over the reward to Marshall to be divided equally with Constable Cummins.[14] Since White had not been convicted of robbing the U.S. mail, this transaction also would cause complications later for the Post Office Department. Now that he was in prison, the government temporarily abandoned their investigation but, in time, they would revive their pursuit of him regardless of their mistakes.

In marked contrast with his arrest, White displayed cleverness and ingenuity during his imprisonment at Yuma. Put to work in the broom department, he learned the trade of making walking canes. By desire and determination he became highly proficient at the craft and was soon put in charge of the entire department. He convinced the prison officials, just as he had done at the West Virginia Penitentiary, to carry on his trade after regular working hours to earn additional money for himself.

Improbable as it sounds, White developed a thriving business inside the prison walls. He began a marketing system, sending his wares to different firms to sell for him and, through confederates at the prison, arranged to have some of the articles he made raffled and sold for large prices. The money came rolling in and he not only stockpiled his earnings but also sent money to his wife in Texas.[15]

The key motive behind White's industry, of course, was freedom. After he had saved up several hundred dollars he contacted the law firm of Baker and Campbell in Phoenix, the leading criminal lawyers in Arizona, to help him obtain a pardon. The attorneys did their job well. A petition requesting White's pardon was circulated throughout Pinal County and was duly signed by many of the residents. By early January, 1891 the attorneys approached acting Territorial Governor of Arizona, N. Oakes Murphy, with the pardon request. The grounds for the pardon were based on the restitution of the money taken from the U.S. mail, White's industry and diligent support of his wife in Texas while still in prison, and the Pinal County petition.[16]

A major factor, however, favorable to White's endeavors in seeking his release was the badly overcrowded conditions at the prison. Conditions became so severe in 1891 that Superintendent Murry McInernay informed the Governor in his Biennial report:

> . . . owing to the overcrowded conditions in the cell-house, which during the summer months was very severe upon the prisoners, it was necessary to excavate additional cellroom from the bank in proximity to the new Hospital, and five roomy and well ventilated cells were constructed in addition to those already built for the accommodation of female prisoners.

During this period of time pardons were readily granted in Arizona due to these conditions. By 1896 the newspapers were sarcastically referring to this procedure as "the Territorial pardon mill."[17]

As a result, after serving only two years and one month of his twelve-year sentence, White was officially pardoned by acting Governor Murphy on January 20, 1891 and released from prison the same day.[18] Through favorable conditions and with the help of his attorneys, White shrewdly gained his precious freedom for the third time. If the officials had known he was the notorious highwayman Ham White, he would not have gained his liberty quite so easily.

Leaving Yuma, White headed directly for California. On the twenty-sixth of January he entered J.W. Bartell's Cane Shop on Commercial Street in Los Angeles. Although Bartell had been a distributor for the canes White made while in prison, he did not know him personally. He introduced himself as Henry Miller, the man who produced and sent the canes from Yuma. When Bartell questioned him about his release from prison, the ex-convict showed him his pardon papers. Bartell agreed to sell White's handicraft and to let him receive mail at the shop.[19]

For the next month White worked industriously, making a number of elegant canes. While in prison he proved that he had the talent to produce excellent products and successfully conduct a business, organizing a profitable and flourishing marketing outlet for his merchandise. Now that he was out of prison he devised a plan in which he sent his products to prominent men across the country, informing them that they could remit to him any amount they deemed sufficient. One of these men, the great orator Colonel Robert G. Ingersoll, was so pleased with his cane that he sent White ten dollars as payment.[20]

On February 25 White informed Bartell that he was going to Santa Barbara and would be gone about three days. Honest toil would not satisfy the unreformed bandit so, instead, he headed north to Shasta County where the stage coach still ran regular routes through the rugged mountainous areas.[21]

For the first time in his career White met armed resistance during a stage robbery. At 7:30 on the evening of March 7 he attempted to rob the stage from Weaverville to Redding on the old Shasta road at a point called the "Double S," about one mile outside of Redding.

Stage driver Ed Graham had all he could handle trying to make headway with the slow moving stagecoach as one of the thorough straps had broken. As the stage reached a slight incline at a bend in the road, Graham was startled by a command to stop. First thinking that one of the four passengers had spoken, Graham and shotgun messenger H.C. Ward looked backward and spotted a masked bandit about ten feet way, crouching behind an oak tree with his pistol pointed at them.

Ward quickly raised his shotgun and, taking aim at the bandit, pulled the trigger but it failed to discharge. Sighting the shotgun and discerning the danger it represented, White screamed at the messenger, "God damn you, I'll shoot!" Ignoring White's threat Ward pulled the trigger again only to have it misfire for the second time. This was too much for the alarmed highwayman and he fired at the coach, shooting twice and wounding the driver in the right side, four inches under the armpit.

By this time Ward got his revolver into play and took a wild shot at White. It was to no avail for, as the messenger fired, the team of horses carried the stage out of sight of the robber.[22]

The driver, whose wound was not serious, drove the stage at a wild run into Redding. The passengers had gotten a good look at the robber and reported him to be a short, slender man wearing a light grey mask. One passenger related that he thought the bandit had been hurt because of the way he moved, not realizing that his stride was due to a lame right leg.

The local officials allowed no one to go to the robbery scene for fear that evidence would be obliterated and hinder any efforts to track the robber. But White, shocked at the consequences of the blundered robbery attempt, had panicked and quickly headed south to Sacramento.[23]

On receiving news of the attempted robbery, Wells Fargo's detectives immediately began an investigation. According to Captain John N. Thacker in an interview with *The Los Angeles Times*: "We took hold and investigated the case carefully. We had a clue on which we were working and by which we had traced the robber to the south towards Sacramento." But the officers were too late as White had left the area.[24]

By 1891 the stagecoach had virtually disappeared, mainly operating in the most remote and rugged areas of the country or as end-of-track service for the railroads. With this in mind, White had studied the stage routes and knew when valuables were to be shipped since the stage he attempted to rob was on the so-called treasure trip. Within a week White regained his composure and again headed north to Redding, determined to hold up the Weaverville-Redding stage.[25]

On March 19, at the exact time and place of his initial robbery,

White stopped the stagecoach for the second time. Fearing another encounter with a shotgun messenger, he took the precaution of hiding behind a larger oak tree and concealing his legs and hips with brush. Unknown to the wary bandit, his cover was unnecessary as no shotgun messenger rode the stage that evening.

There were two passengers inside the stage and a young woman, a Miss Osgood of Weaverville, who sat topside with the stage driver. As the stage approached the scene of the previous robbery attempt, driver Ed Brackett began relating a detailed account of the whole affair to the young woman. Reaching the exact site of the holdup, Brackett pointed it out to her. She anxiously moved closer to the driver and exclaimed, "I hate this place."

At almost the precise moment Miss Osgood uttered her words, a harsh command of "Stop! Stop! Stop!" rang out, nearly causing the already frightened young woman to leap out of her seat. Jerking the horses to a standstill and looking backward, the driver saw the gleam of a six-shooter being held by a bandit partially hidden behind a large oak tree. The bandit's head and shoulders were covered by a gunnysack and the revolver was shaking in his hand.

Unable to forget his previous confrontation with the shotgun messenger, White could not stop the trembling in his hand. Although he had several masks in his possession, in his anxiety, he discarded the idea of holding up the passengers. Nevertheless, he intended to go through with the robbery and told the driver to throw out the box. Brackett immediately complied, throwing out a small box.

Through White's experience with stage robbery he knew additional express boxes were on board. Regaining his confidence, he ordered the driver to throw out the big box, which also was quickly obeyed. Being informed that there was nothing else on board, White told Brackett to drive on.[26]

The following report from *The Los Angeles Times*, outlined the excitement and furor the robbery provoked:

> The stage came into Redding on the dead run and the alarm was given. A large posse of men and officers started immediately in pursuit. It was ascertained positively that the robber is the same man who held up the stage on the 7 th instant.[27]

Immediately following the robbery, Wells Fargo detectives hurried to Redding and according to Captain Thacker:

We investigated the robbery after it occurred. In looking over the field we found twelve masks buried about 100 feet from where the stage was stopped. The box had been broken open in a way which indicated that an amateur had done it. This was only a decoy . . .[28]

White's booty amounted to around fifty dollars worth of retort gold and several smaller gold nuggets knows as "chispas." Confident and satisfied with his success he headed south. Reaching Sacramento, he took time to purchase a new suit of clothes from Lewis Brothers at 231 K Street before boarding the Frisco train for Los Angeles.[29]

CHAPTER EIGHT

The Only Safe Place For Such A Man As Him Is Behind Bars — He Is One Of The Shrewdest, Slickest Men In His Line I Have Ever Come Across

Arriving in Los Angeles on Sunday morning, March 22, White went directly to Bartell's Cane Shop to collect his mail. During the conversation with Bartell, he claimed that he had been delayed in Santa Barbara and offered to go to Santa Monica and trim some trees for the shop owner. In his mail White found a registered letter informing him to pick up a package at Postal Station C, the Pico House, unaware that it was a decoy.

Unknown to White, the U.S. Post Office Department had learned that he had been pardoned from prison and immediately revived their investigation. On March 1 U.S. Marshal George E. Gard in Los Angeles received word from the Postal authorities that the wanted man was thought to be somewhere in the city. Following leads, the officers traced him to Bartell's Cane Shop. When questioned by U.S. Deputy Marshal A.W. Marsh, Bartell told him that White had left Los Angeles for Santa Barbara on February 27 and that his mail was being delivered at the cane shop until he returned. After a cursory check in Santa Barbara the officers determined that he had never been there. Since Bartell was holding White's mail, the officers concluded that their best course of action would be to wait until he returned to Los Angeles.

Marshal Gard, a shrewd lawman, outlined a plan to trap White. Gard and Marsh prepared and mailed the decoy registered letter to Bartell's shop and patiently waited for the wanted man's arrival.

Early Monday morning White entered Station C and went to the postal window to pick up his package. Through information obviously supplied by Bartell, U.S. Marshal Frank P. Flint and Deputy Sheriff

Billy Hammell were waiting for him when he arrived. As White signed for his package the two officers stepped up and arrested him.

At first White seemed surprised but quickly regained his composure and took his arrest in a matter-of-fact way. At the U.S. Marshal's office the officers immediately began questioning him. White told them that after leaving Los Angeles he had gone to Ventura to work for a friend, but refused to give the friend's name. He then stated that he had returned to Los Angeles to collect some money owed to him by former inmates he had known in prison but stubbornly refused to give the officers any further information.

Searching White and discovering the retort gold and five or six small gold nuggets the officers began to suspect him of the Weaverville-Redding stage holdup. When questioned, he adamantly denied any connection with the robbery. Probably intending to mislead his interrogators, White stated that he thought he had been arrested for shooting a man in Texas. If he believed this would distract the officers he was badly mistaken. This was a lead that the officers should have pursued, but they were more interested in the contents of his pockets.

Upon finding the gold, Marshal Gard concluded that it was necessary to check White's baggage. White refused to reveal where it was, stating only that it was in safe hands, so Gard sent Marsh to search for it. In short order he discovered that the suspected bandit had a room at the St. Charles Hotel, 25 North Main Street. Searching the room, he found the baggage which contained the following items: a pair of heavy red woolen underwear which would be worn only in the northern part of the country; a .41 calibre Colt revolver and eight cartridges; a pocket compass; and, most important of all, an old suit of clothing in a wrapping-paper marked "Lewis Brothers, 231 K Street, Sacramento, Cal." plus a paper with the name, "Charles E. Hager, Lathrop, Cal." This evidence proved to the officer that their prisoner had unquestionably gone north instead of to Ventura. Another confirming bit of evidence, undoubtedly furnished by Bartell, was that White did not have over twenty dollars on his person when he left Los Angeles.

After the interrogation the marshals locked White up in the Los Angeles County jail on a complaint made by a Deputy U. S. Marshal in Arizona, charging him with the 1888 mail robbery. Confining him to the empty female ward, the officers allowed no one to communicate with him. Since Wells Fargo had been investigating the Weaverville-

Redding stage robbery, Marshal Gard immediately contacted Captain John Thacker, Assistant Chief of the Detective Bureau in San Francisco, informing him of White's arrest.[1]

Now the whirlwind started in full. The local newspapers picked up the story and White again became headline news — a carbon copy of the Denver period ten years before. *The Los Angeles Times* gave the story the most attention but, unlike the Denver newspapers, they stretched the truth in their reports on Henry Miller, completely ignorant of his true identity. The *Times* began their reporting on March 29 and for several days continued the story with such headlines as:

> March 29 — "Another Black Bart"
> March 30 — "Lone Highwayman"
> April 1 — "Miller Is The Man"
> April 5 — "Miller The Highwayman Held to Answer"

Because of the publicity devoted to White's arrest in *The Times*, the U.S. Marshal's office received a flood of telegrams requesting information about the lone highwayman. Evidently some of the telegrams were from Texas as the *Times* reported their prisoner was suspected of committing several stagecoach robberies in that state, undoubtedly referring to the "lone highwayman" robberies near Ballinger. The evidence, however, was not sufficient enough to indict him.[2] Had the marshals known who Henry Miller actually was, they could have had him indicted on Federal charges in Texas, but the connection was never made and White remained Henry Miller.

As mentioned, the *Times* gave an account of Henry Miller's background. Apparently they were not satisfied with the news at hand so they concocted a fictitious career for the bandit, fed it to the public, and played it up for all it was worth. Here is the tale, word for word, printed by the *Times*:

A PREVIOUS RECORD

The first heard of Miller was during the years 1885, 1886, and 1887 in the territories of Idaho and Montana. He established throughout that region an enviable record as a successful, enterprising, and daring stage robber.

But finally like all others engaged in that line of business, Miller became involved in a dispute with a driver of a stage he had stopped. In the melee Miller was shot in the right knee, he was then overpowered and captured. He was heavily ironed but was never landed in jail. The same night of the day that he was captured he managed to file the chains which held his legs together. He then escaped and traveled for over 100 miles with the irons still on his legs. In some way he succeeded in getting rid of them altogether and fled to Texas.

Here Miller created a sensation. He became involved in a quarrel, and a shooting scrape was the result, in which Miller escaped but a man was shot.[3]

Since White was in the penitentiary from 1881 until January of 1887 and did not adopt the alias of Henry Miller until mid-1887, the *Times* could have had him mixed up with someone else. However, the entire content of the story is suspect, especially the part where the bandit is able to file through his leg irons while being guarded, escape from his captors in Montana and **walk one hundred miles with a bullet in his knee the same night he was shot.**

The story is so implausible that a competitive newspaper, *The Los Angeles Herald*, investigated the whole affair and reported their findings:

Policemen, detectives and patrolmen looked at one another in amazement yesterday, when they read in the Times about the clever and remarkable capture of one Henry Miller by Marshal Gard and several of his deputies. Miller is called a second Black Bart — another Claude Duval — and is reported to have a record of crime which reads like a romance. Marshal Gard is credited with having placed behind bars a most dangerous criminal, and the marshal and his deputies are congratulated upon the adroit and sagacious way in which they effected the capture.

Henry Miller was arrested in this city last Monday by a deputy United States marshal. At the request of the marshal no record of the arrest was made on the register at the jail. Jailer Pallett was also requested not to make known the fact of the arrest. The authorities at the county jail were faithful to their trust, but one of the deputies connected with the marshal's office got in his deadly work on a Times reporter, and in consequence, the readers of that paper with treated with a fairy tale.[4]

Unwilling to retract the story, *The Times* made these comments to the rebuttal:

The story of Miller's life for the past eight years, as printed Sunday morning in connection with the announcement of his capture, aroused

Artist's sketch of Ham White, as Henry Miller, as it appeared in *The Los Angeles Times*, March 29, 1891.

the envy of a morning contemporary. Yesterday, the contemporary referred to the whole thing as a "fairy tale." Despite this every detail of Miller's record, as printed, was true.[5]

One wonders how the public accepted this "fairy tale," as *The Herald* so aptly named it or, for that matter, how White reacted to all this hoopla. The newspapers would have really had a field day if they had known that Miller was in reality the Texas stage robber, Ham White.

Receiving the information of White's arrest, Captain Thacker of

Wells Fargo wired Marshal Gard on March 30 asking if any retort gold had been found on the bandit. Gard immediately wired in the affirmative and received a return telegram that Thacker was coming to Los Angeles at once.

At the same time Post Office Inspector M.H. Flint in Los Angeles sent a special letter to Inspector George L. Seybolt in San Francisco informing him of the arrest of "Henry Miller." The next day, March 30, Inspector Seybolt telegraphed the following to the postmaster at Los Angeles: "Have Gard hold Miller at all hazards until I arrive."

White's preliminary examination in U.S. Commissioners Court for the 1888 Arizona mail robbery had been scheduled for March 31 but was postponed until April 4 in order to give Inspector Seybolt a chance to concentrate and examine all the information surrounding the case, thus preventing him from coming to Los Angeles as planned. However, Captain Thacker, who was only interested in the Weaverville-Redding stage robbery, arrived by train at 7:30 AM on March 31. He immediately went to the county jail to interview White but Gard was out of town and he had to wait until the marshal returned at 2 PM.

Brought to the Marshal's office, White was questioned by Gard and Thacker for two solid hours. Reluctant to make any statements, he avoided speaking with the officers as much as possible. Unknown to the prisoner, arrangements had been made to photograph him during the interview. To White this was a breach of his rules and he flew into a rage, angrily protesting their deviousness. His objections were in vain; however, he did have the satisfaction of knowing that the officers gained nothing from the interrogation but his photograph.[6]

Two months later, in an interview with a reporter from *The Arizona Weekly Enterprise*, White gave the only account revealing the details of his interrogation by Gard and Thacker:

> When I was under arrest in Los Angeles, Marshal Gard and detective Thacker accused me of robbing stages in that state. I denied the charges and pleaded with them to let me stand trial in California before I should be brought back to Arizona, for I knew well such reports, false though they were, would do me injury unless I could have a chance to prove myself innocent. They said no; not unless I would consent to plead guilty, and if I would do that, they would take me up to Redding, and also, they could get me off with a light sentence, and unless I did consent to plead guilty, they would take me back to Arizona where I would be

sent to some eastern prison for life. I told them I did not think I would be sent up for life, as the people there knew I had been punished once for the same crime, and they had some sympathy for me; they only laughed at this, and said with all these bad reports against me, I would be disappointed in that respect. I said I thought not, as the Judge I would be tried before knew something about newspaper reports. They laughed at this and said, I would have to have something more than that to contend against.[7]

Examining the retort gold taken from White, Captain Thacker positively identified each piece as having been stolen from the express box during the Weaverville-Redding stage robbery. In an interview with a *Los Angeles Times* reporter, Thacker made these comments about the bandit:

"There is now no doubt," said the Captain. "Miller is the Black Bart who robbed the Weaverville stage. Not only this. He is one of the most dangerous and daring stage robbers who have infested the Pacific slope for the past ten years. I myself have known him for the past five years or so. The only safe place for such a man as him is behind bars. He is one of the shrewdest, slickest men in his line I have ever come across."[8]

Either the *Times* had misquoted Thacker or he stretched the truth in stating he had known White "for the past five years of so," as only two and a half years had passed since the Arizona stage holdup.

The interrogation and all the publicity worried White and he immediately sought help from the law firm that had obtained his pardon from the prison at Yuma. Shortly after the interrogation *The Los Angeles Times* interviewed him and gave the following report:

Miller himself admits the officers have him in a hole, and he was really debating what to do. . . . That Miller recognizes the predicament he is in is shown by the fact that he yesterday telegraphed his lawyers, Baker and Campbell of Phoenix, Ariz. This firm comprises the two best criminal lawyers in Arizona.[9]

Apparently the Arizona law firm had had enough of White's antics. Only two months after they had obtained his pardon from Yuma he was involved in another stage robbery and again behind bars. Representing the bandit now would not benefit their reputation so the firm completely ignored his plea for help.

The mistakes the Post Office Department made after White's arrest and conviction in 1888 now came back to haunt them. Inspector Seybolt fully realized this after examining the records. Their major concern was duplicating the charge on which White had been convicted in 1888 and ending up having the case dismissed. Also, the Department had issued a reward for White's conviction on the charge of robbing the U.S. mail and the reward had been duly paid. Since White had not been convicted for robbing the U.S. mail, this weakened the government's case. Another issue that troubled Seybolt was White's claim that in December, 1888 Inspector Herbert promised him that if he returned the money taken from the U.S. mail he would not be prosecuted by the government. White made good the restitution of the money.

In his frustration Inspector Seybolt sent numerous letters and telegrams to various Postal authorities and other government officials requesting advice and instruction on how to proceed with the case. After analyzing all of the information, Seybolt seriously doubted that White could be convicted in a U.S. Court for robbing the U.S. mail. Emphasizing these fears, he telegraphed Chief Post Office Inspector E.G. Rathbone in Washington, D.C. on April 2, and followed it with a letter the next day recommending that White be turned over to the California authorities. Seybolt assured Rathbone that Wells Fargo had an absolute case against White for the Weaverville-Redding robberies and, if tried for this crime he would unquestionably be convicted.

On receipt of the telegram Chief Inspector Rathbone examined all the available information concerning the case and sent his findings by letter to Seybolt on April 3. In his reply, Rathbone advised Seybolt to proceed with the case, assuring him that White had clearly been convicted on a Territorial charge and not for robbing the U.S. mails.

On April 8, after receiving Rathbone's letter, Seybolt directed Deputy Post Office Inspector W.A. Robinson of the Los Angeles office to gather all pertinent facts and make a report as to the feasibility of bringing White to trial on the charge of robbing the U.S. mail. For the entire month of April and the first part of May these investigations and inquiries continued. As a result the U.S. Post Office decided to proceed with their legal action against White. Their assumption was that White had been previously convicted on the charge of robbing Dr. Hurley. This assumption was incorrect as he had been convicted for robbing the express box, but it was irrelevant as both charges fell under Territorial jurisdiction.[10]

While incarcerated in the Los Angeles County jail White continued to deny his involvement in the Weaverville-Redding stage robbery. On the other hand, because of his previous confession, trial, and conviction, he had no choice but to admit to the 1888 Arizona stage holdup. He reasoned that because of his prior conviction he stood a good chance of having the case dismissed. The Weaverville-Redding affair was another matter entirely for if he confessed to that holdup he certainly would be convicted. Even without his confession, White knew that Wells Fargo had assured the U.S. Postal authorities that they had an absolute case against him.[11] He decided he would much rather take his chances in United States Court.

On the morning of April 4 White had his preliminary examination before U.S. Commissioner Van Dyke. Dr. Hurley, as an eyewitness to the crime of robbing the U.S. mail, gave his testimony. Following Hurley, Marshal Gard and Deputy Marshal Marsh testified that in their presence the prisoner had confessed to robbing the U.S. mail. White was not represented by counsel and made no statement whatsoever. Based on the evidence presented, the Court ordered that he be held pending trial in U.S. District Court in the Territory of Arizona on the charge of robbing the U.S. mail and assaulting the stage driver. His bail was set at five thousand dollars. Unable to raise bond, he was turned over to the U.S. Marshal's office to be conveyed to Arizona.

The officers wasted no time in transferring the prisoner out of their jurisdiction. At 5:10 PM on the same day, April 4, White left Los Angeles for Arizona in the custody of U.S. Marshal George Gard.[12]

PART III

His Race is Now Run

CHAPTER NINE

All is Over. I Send You $50.00. Goodbye.

U.S. Marshall George Gard delivered his prisoner without incident to the authorities in Florence, Arizona and White again experienced confinement in the Pinal County jail. Suspecting that he was in league with other outlaws in Arizona and California, Postal Inspector Robinson from the Los Angeles office, U.S. District Attorney Thomas F. Wilson, and Dr. Hurley interviewed White in jail a few days before his scheduled trial date of May 14. The only account of this meeting was White's version, which was printed in *The Florence Enterprise*:

> I was told that if I would give information against other parties I might then expect mercy from court, and if I did not do something to help the law abiding people, it was useless for me to hope for mercy; and in spite of my protestations that I knew nothing against anyone, I could not make them believe I was telling the truth. At that interview Mr. Robinson referred several times to robberies committed in California and other places. I saw what his object was, and finally I asked him if I was being prosecuted for those crimes. He said no. Then I asked him if it was just for him to come here and try to prejudice the people against me, on account of those crimes, crimes which I did not commit.[1]

By mid-May the Postal authorities were ready to proceed with their case against White. On the fourteenth he was brought before the grand jury in U.S. District Court, Second Judicial District for the Territory of Arizona in Florence, and indicted on three separate charges.

Conducting a thorough review of White's previous case, District Attorney Wilson drew up charges that would not conflict with White's prior conviction. In Case Number 206, the court indicted White for robbing a person entrusted with the U.S. mail and in Case Numbers

207 and 230, for robbing a person entrusted with the mail and putting the life of said person in jeopardy by the use of a dangerous weapon. After the grand jury indictments, he was arraigned and the court appointed W.H. Griffin and Francis J. Henley as defense counsel. Stating to the court that Henry Miller was his true name, White was granted one day to enter a plea.[2]

On May 15 White returned to court which was presided over by Judge Joseph Kibbey. Before a plea was entered for Case Numbers 206 and 207, the defense responded and objected to the charges on the following grounds:

I. That the indictment does not substantially conform to the requirements of sections 1457–1458 and 1459 of the Penal Code of Arizona; II. That the indictment is not direct and certain as to the offense charged; III. That the indictment is not direct and certain as regards the particular circumstances of the offense charged; and IV. That the indictment does not state facts sufficient to constitute the offense charged in that it fails to allege a taking and carrying away of the property alleged to have been forcibly stolen.

The attorneys' objections were overruled by Judge Kibbey and White pled not guilty to the charges. Trial date was set for May 19.[3]

On the first day of trial White's attorneys were again overruled when they entered a second response to the indictments. Playing for time, the defense requested a continuance which was denied and a jury was impaneled for Case Number 206. After the indictments were read to the jury, the prosecution called LeBarron, Hurley, Saxe, and Postmaster John Miller to testify. Following their testimony, the defense counsel stated that they had no evidence to offer. The case was argued by the attorneys and then submitted to the jury. Wasting no time, the jury under foreman George Campbell brought in a verdict of guilty on the same day. Judge Kibbey set the following day, May 20, as the date of sentencing.

White's fear of prejudice came to pass as evidenced by the jury's quick decision, which was obviously influenced by the California stage robberies he had committed. The jury members, all Pinal County residents, were well aware of the petition circulated in Pinal County that helped obtain his pardon from Yuma and had been sympathetic to his cause at the time. They realized they had been duped and rectified their mistake by a quick verdict. If White had not robbed the Weaverville-Redding stage he might well have gone free.

For some reason the court allowed the date of sentencing to be postponed until May 25. Before sentence could be passed, White's defense counsel submitted a plea of former conviction to bar further prosecution in Case Number 207. Judge Kibbey took the plea under advisement. On a motion by the district attorney, sentencing was again postponed until the following day.

On the twenty-sixth, U.S. Attorney Wilson entered *nolle prosequi* (unwilling to prosecute) in Case Number 207 and the case was dismissed. As to White's sentence, Judge Kibbey rendered the following judgment: "It is therefore ordered, adjudged and decreed. And the judgment and sentence of the Court is, that you, Henry Miller, be punished by imprisonment in the State Prison of California at San Quentin at hard labor, for a term of Ten Years, to date from 26th May AD 1891." White was placed in custody of Deputy U.S. Marshal John V. Paul to be delivered to San Quentin. Strangely, Case Number 230 was not dismissed until February 6, 1893.[4]

White felt the major cause of his predicament was not the jury or Judge Kibbey, but the avenging Dr. J.M. Hurley. Passing Hurley outside the courtroom after his sentencing, he suddenly stopped and, in a rage, told the doctor that if he lived to get out of prison he would hunt him down and kill him. After a week White's temper cooled and he realized that his statements would do him more harm than good. He made an apology and explained the reason for his anger in a statement to *The Arizona Enterprise*:

FLORENCE JAIL, June 3, 1891

EDITOR ENTERPRISE: — In the *Enterprise* of May 30th there is an item about what I said to Dr. Hurley on returning to jail after receiving my sentence. I was sorry I made such foolish remarks in less than five minutes after the words were spoken. I have not the least bit of hard feeling for Mr. Saxe nor Mr. LeBarron for testifying against me, for they only testified to what they believed to be true; but is different in Dr. Hurley's case, he was not content to come here and give in his evidence alone; if he had been, I could not have blamed him for doing so. But I know he did everything he could do to make the U.S. Attorney believe that I was in league with other criminals in Arizona and elsewhere, and if I would I could give information that would lead to the arrest and conviction of several other parties who have been robbing stages here in Arizona and other parts of the country.

How well he succeeded in not only convincing Mr. Wilson that I was one of the worst men that have ever been in Arizona, is evident from the very severe sentence I received.[5]

White had an inordinate fear of being incarcerated at San Quentin and immediately sought legal action to help him obtain a transfer to another penitentiary. On June 8, from the Pinal County jail, he wrote a letter to U.S. Attorney General Miller in Washington, D.C. requesting a transfer to the Arizona Territorial Penitentiary at Yuma. He based his request on the grounds that during his imprisonment at Yuma he had been allowed to work on his own time to earn money to support his family and he would not be able to do this at San Quentin.

He added a few other comments in his letter to strengthen his case, such as the promise of immunity alleged to have been given him by Inspector Herbert for restitution of the money and the fact that Judge Kibbey refused to allow him either witnesses or the presentation of this evidence to the jury. He also complained that no U.S. indictment had been found against him while he was at Yuma or when the U.S. authorities became aware of his pardon petition, but, as soon as he was pardoned, a U.S. warrant was issued for his arrest. Apprehensively, he wrote that he expected to be taken to San Quentin around July 1 and appealed to the Attorney General to grant his request and send instructions to U.S. Marshal Paul at once.[6] But White's timing was off and he was scheduled to be transferred to San Quentin much sooner than he anticipated.

On June 10 Marshal Paul and Pinal County Sheriff W.C. Truman removed White from the Florence jail and took him to Casa Grande to await the train to San Francisco. Constable D.W. Cummins, who had captured the bandit after the 1888 stage robbery, joined the two lawmen upon their arrival at Casa Grande. The officers, unfamiliar with White's previous history, were totally unaware of his determination to avoid imprisonment at San Quentin. Their laxity gave White his chance and he pulled off the greatest escape of his career. It was a daring move, yet tinged with humor, just like a page out of a dime-novel thriller.

The three officers arranged to spend the night's lodging in a dwelling near the railroad station. Cots were set up with White sandwiched between Sheriff Truman and Marshal Paul while Constable Cummins was on guard outside the door. Later that night, after the two officers were asleep, Cummins came in and sat down on his cot. White waited until the constable was drowsing and then carefully arose from his cot. Wrapping his shackles in a sheet to prevent making any noise, he stealthily made his way towards the doorway.

With mixed feelings of need and derisive humor, White passed by the sheriff's cot, cautiously leaned over the sleeping man and took his watch and money. Making his way to the door, he passed so close to Cummins that his chest barely touched the officer's back, miraculously without waking him. Passing safely through the doorway, White hurried to a blacksmith shop where he took a piece of iron and a canteen of water. He went directly to the railroad tracks, broke the chains on his leg irons, and headed into the desert on foot.

White walked all night in the direction of Sacaton, crossing dry lakes and skirting mountains. He had been fooled by the weight of the canteen as it held little water and was soon empty. By the next day his thirst became so unbearable that he bit into his own flesh and drank the blood. Believing that he was going to die, White's thoughts turned to his wife and he drafted the following two notes:

Mr. Paul — Please send this money by Wells, Fargo and Co.'s express to

> Mrs. NANIE MILLER
> DUFFAU
> VIA HEIR, TEXAS

DARLING NANNIE:

All is over. I send you $50.00. Goodbye

HENRY

Not quite giving up, White wandered several hours until he found a waterhole near the Gila River and drank so much he became ill, forcing him to remain there most of the day. Although sick and weary he finally managed to continue on, traveling in circles until he stumbled upon a ranch owned by a man named Walker. Finding no one at home, he laid down and went to sleep. Later that day the rancher returned and, even though he did not know White, allowed him to stay the night and gave him breakfast the next morning, June 12. Telling Walker he was going to Florence, he headed in that direction for two and a half miles and then changed course to throw any followers off his track.

Three hired men from Walker's ranch received information from a nearby rancher named Morse about White's escape and that a reward of $100 was being offered for his capture. They immediately started in pursuit. Although White had changed direction, the three men soon came in sight of him. Realizing the intent of his three pursuers, and being unarmed, he tried to fight them off by throwing rocks at them. Not wanting to kill the fugitive, the three men easily overpowered and captured him because of his weakened condition. They immediately took him to Florence and turned him over to Marshal Paul that evening.[7]

After this embarrassing episode, the chagrined Marshal Paul took no more chances with White and hustled him aboard the train for San Francisco. The marshal kept a close watch over his prisoner and delivered him safely to the San Francisco City jail on June 15.[8]

Without any delay White was transferred to San Quentin the same day and registered as Henry Miller, Convict no. 14579. Three separate photographs were taken of White, two with a full beard and civilian clothing and one after he was shaved and in prison garb. The following statistics were recorded: Convict No. 14579; Name — Henry Miller; Nativity — Texas; Crime — robbery U.S. mail carrier; Received — June 15, 1891; Sentenced to ten years, from U.S.D. Arizona; 38 years old; Broom maker; 5'9 7/8" tall; Weight — 150 lbs.; Florid complexion; Light grey eyes; Thin and light hair; Notation: Served term in Yuma Arizona for same offense from December, 1888 to January, 1891, pardoned.[9]

White persistently continued his efforts to obtain a transfer out of San Quentin. On October 28, just four months after his imprisonment, he wrote another letter to the Attorney General reminding him of his first letter written in June. He again requested a transfer to Yuma even though he claimed there was less work and better food at San Quentin. He wrote that he wanted the reassignment so he would "be able to help those who have a right to look to him for help" and again alluded to the Postal Inspector's promise of not prosecuting him if the money stolen from the U.S. mail was returned. Taking a different course, he blamed Republican law officers for not honoring the promises of Democratic

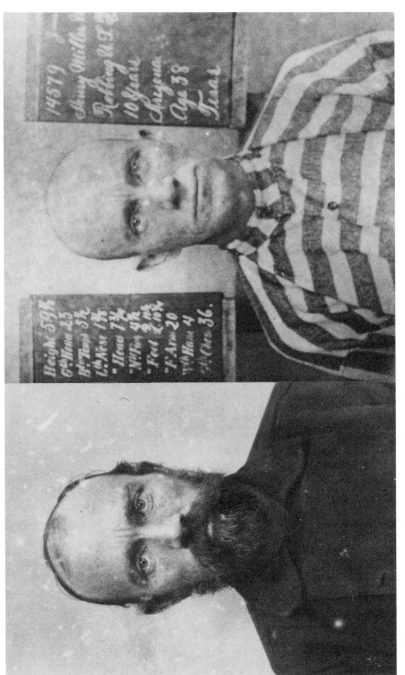

San Quentin Prison photographs of Ham White, as Henry Miller, taken in 1891. Photograph on right was taken after White was shaved of all facial hair. Courtesy: California State Archives, Sacramento, California.

officers. In desperation, White even requested permission to be tried for the Weaverville-Redding stage robbery, stating he was innocent of that crime.[10]

Not hearing from the Attorney General within a month, White wrote a third letter on November 26 from Cell no. 11. In this letter he expressed frustration and restrained anger, reminding the Attorney General of his two previous letters and requesting assurance that they had been received. In a terse sentence he remarked, "If you have received them and have decided not to do anything for me I will be very glad if you will return the papers I sent from the Florence Jail, as they may be of use to me when Grover Cleveland gets back in the White House." White requested a speedy trial date for the Weaverville-Redding stage robbery and ended the letter with the mild threat, "Or will it be necessary for me to spend the last dollar I have in the world to employ counsel to answer these questions, which I will have to do if you will not write to me."[11]

This last letter did get results although it was not to White's liking. On December 3 the Attorney General sent the following letter to U.S. Attorney H.R. Jeffords in Tucson, Arizona:

> Enclosed is a letter from one Henry Miller, a United States prisoner now confined in the California State Prison at San Quentin. He asks to be transferred to the Territorial Penitentiary at Yuma, Arizona, and also complains of the treatment he received at the time of his conviction. I desire from you a report concerning these matters.[12]

Jeffords turned this letter over to U.S. District Attorney Wilson, the prosecuting attorney during White's trial. On December 23 Wilson sent the requested report to the Attorney General, outlining White's criminal career in Arizona and California in a fair and accurate manner. He stated that no promises of immunity from prosecution for mail robbery had been made to the prisoner by any Post Office Inspector. In his summation, Wilson stated:

> Miller is one of the most expert and daring Mail and Stage Robbers West of the Rocky Mountains.
> I am satisfied that Miller's object in asking to be transferred from San Quentin to Yuma, is to afford him an opportunity to escape in transit, and if failing in that to earn something with which to employ persons to aid him in getting out of prison.
> His claim that he wants to earn money to "be able to help those who

have a right to look to him for help" is in my opinion false, for the reason that Ex-Sheriff Fryer of Florence under whose charge Miller was in jail informs me Miller abandoned his wife and family some years ago in Texas.

I have gone into the particulars of the case because there are no mitigating circumstances in Miller's case, and he is an old and experienced criminal too dangerous to be allowed the least opportunity of an escape, in being transferred from San Quentin to Yuma and besides I believe that the main reason why Miller wants to be at Yuma is because the prisoners are worked outside the prison, which affords an additional chance of escape.[13]

And that bit of formidable writing put the lid on any positive action the Attorney General might have granted in White's behalf. He had finally entered a penitentiary in which he could not gain his freedom through manipulation. Therefore, he resigned himself to follow the regulations and quietly serve out his sentence. San Quentin's merit system, based on the Goodman Act of 1880, allowed a prisoner serving a ten-year sentence to be released after six years and six months. Following all the rules and regulations, White was released on December 26, 1897, having served a little over six years and six months of his sentence.[14]

Letters to this grade must be signed in full.

Each prisoner may be allowed to correspond with his own immediate friends and relatives once in two weeks, and no oftener, except in case of serious illness, and he may be visited, by permission of the Warden. For any violation of the rules, the privilege of correspondence will be withdrawn. Packages of Tobacco, Fruit, Food, or Wearing Apparel, sent to prisoners, will not be admitted. Letters in cipher will be destroyed. No Prisoner will be permitted to manufacture articles on their own account, to be sold or to be sent out to friends, or to be bartered in any way.

Post Office Address: SAN QUENTIN PRISON, Marin Co., Cal.,

No. *14574*, Cell *11*   *November 26, 1891*

United States Attorney General
Washington D.C.

Dear Sir

I have written you two letters in regard to my case, but have not received an answer from either of them, It may be you did not receive the letters and papers I sent you, let that be as it may I do hope you will write to me so that I may know if you received them or not. If you have received them, and have decided not to do any thing for me I will be very glad if you will return the papers I sent from Florence jail, as they may be of use to me when Grover Cleveland gets back in the white house. In my last letter I asked, if you

would let Wells, Fargoes detectives take me out of this prison for tryal on a charge of of robbery that they accuse me of doing. I have more then one reason for wanting a speedy tryal in this case. Among the lesser ones is, that U.S. Marshall Gard has some property that was taken from me when I was arrested, which he holds, as he says, at the request of the detectives as evidence against me Now if you will pleas write me a few lines saying that I can be taken out for tryal, every thing will be all right. If the law is such that I cant be taken out untill I have served my time out. I would be very if you would inform me. or will it be necessary for me to spend the lost dollar I have in the world to employ counsel to answer these questions, which I will have to do if you will not write to me
Respectfully
Henry Miller

110

CHAPTER TEN

It Will Take Only a Little Money to Do Us The Balance of Our Lives

Leaving San Quentin on that late December day the forty-three-year-old White had many things to contemplate. His primary thoughts centered on his health. While in San Quentin he had contracted the dreaded disease of the 1800s, tuberculosis, and knew there was no cure. White was just one of a high ratio of inmates who caught this disease because of the crowded prison conditions during this period of time.[1]

White also faced the fact that he had robbed his last stagecoach and his glorious days as the lone highwayman were over. Although there were stagecoaches still running regular routes around Shasta, California, he had found out how risky that was after he had robbed the Weaverville-Redding stagecoach. White was now a remnant of the past, a lost breed like the buffalo he had hunted in 1876.

From late December, 1897 through mid-May, 1898 there is no documentation confirming White's whereabouts. Also, there is no evidence whether White kept in contact with his wife during his imprisonment, however, it is possible that he visited her in Erath County after his release. If he did, it was to no avail for White later claimed he was unmarried.

After White left Bastrop County in 1881, his relatives lost all track of him and there are no family records indicating that he returned home after his release from San Quentin.[2] White gave the only account concerning his actions during this period in an interview with a reporter in San Antonio in June of 1898, claiming he had spent most of his time in Nashville, Tennessee.[3] If this was true, he apparently kept out of trouble, likely working at odd jobs at least until May of 1898 when he again shows up in Texas.

During White's ten-year absence drastic changes had taken place in Texas. While the industrial revolution and growth of towns spread across the eastern United States, none of this occurred in Texas. The opening of vast new lands in west Texas brought a deluge of impoverished farmers to the state, but inactive money supply enforced by the gold standard as well as the absence of credit under the Texas homestead law destroyed them before they gained a foothold. In turn, these small farmers and ranchers blamed the railroads and big money monopolies for their plight. The rising protests of these destitute farmers brought on a new type of politician, one who would declare war on big business. Foremost among them was Democrat James Stephen Hogg.

Born near Rusk, Texas in 1851, Hogg rose through the ranks from District Attorney in the Seventh District to State Attorney General by 1886. As the first native-born gubernatorial candidate, Hogg handily won the office in 1890 on the platform of advocating state control of all railroads through a Railroad Commission. Nevertheless, not even Hogg was radical enough for the Farmers' Alliance, a non-partisan agrarian group formed in 1875 at Lampasas. Although the Alliance supported Hogg's policies of abolishing the national banking system, stopping foreign land grants, and free coinage of silver, they demanded more than mere regulation. Consequently the Alliance broke from the Democratic ranks in 1892 and became the backbone of the new founded radical reform party called the Populist or People's Party.

From 1892 to its peak year of 1896 the Populists became a major third party threat to the controlling Democrats and Republicans in Texas. The overwhelming depression of the early 1890s brought about the sudden rise of the Populist movement, and, although they never gained the Governorship of Texas, they succeeded in electing several candidates to the Texas House of Representatives and Senate. The demise of the Populists equalled its abrupt rise. Never having a true ideological foundation, the party based its structure on opposition to the moneyed east and the accrual of hard cash rather than social reform. By the time Ham White returned to Texas in mid-1898, the Populists had all but disappeared; however, the economic outlook for the small farmer had improved. Because of northern urbanization and an improved European market, these farmers now had hard cash in their pockets.[4]

The only change that affected White after his imprisonment was the disappearance of the stagecoach. This had been his main source of livelihood and pleasure during the periods of time he was not in prison. He could make brooms, shoes, and elegant canes but that would not satisfy his lawless nature, so now he would have to devise a new plan to appease this need. By mid-May of 1898 he did just that, deciding to try his hand at train robbery.

On the evening of May 15 White made his strike at the San Antonio and Aransas Pass Railroad about a mile and a quarter from Kenedy, Texas. New at this type of robbery, he had no idea how to stop a train. Working alone, he concluded that the only way to successfully accomplish this would be to obstruct the tracks, forcing the train to stop.

White placed numerous railroad ties on a railroad bridge, dynamited the tracks and roadbed, and then waited for the arrival of the train. Apparently he neglected to check out the railroad schedules since the first train to come through was an eastbound stock train. The whole plan was a fiasco. Dumbfounded, he helplessly watched the train pass over the dynamited areas, crash through the barrier of railroad ties without serious damage, and continue unhindered down the tracks.[5]

Even though the train robbery scheme came to naught, it helped him conceive a new course of action. Since he could not stop and holdup a train alone, White devised an audacious plan to rob the railroad by extortion.

His target, the San Antonio and Aransas Pass Railway, was not much more than a dream when railroad promoter Uriah Lott proposed to build a line from Corpus Christi to San Antonio in 1884. Relying on finances from the cities along the line, Lott secured a charter on August 28, 1884 and by January, 1886 had completed thirty miles of track from San Antonio to Floresville. Running out of funds, Lott's plan was saved by Mifflin Kenedy of Corpus Christi, who took over the building contract and received payment in railroad stocks and bonds.

In five years Kenedy actually completed the laying of 688 miles of track, extending from San Antonio to Alice, Corpus Christi, Rockport, Kerrville, Waco, and Houston. In July of 1890 the company was forced into receivership and much of the stock was acquired by the Southern Pacific Railway. The S.A. and A.P. had become a major competitor of the Southern Pacific so, to eliminate this competition, the new owners worked out a plan with Kenedy that guaranteed his interests which was approved by the receivers and the court.

In June of 1892, to avoid reorganization and rechartering, receivership was terminated and the Southern Pacific took over the line. Although the Southern Pacific now owned a competing line, the Railroad Commission did not enforce regulations against them until 1903, possibly because they operated it as a separate line. Also in 1892, M.D. Monserrate, Vice President of the New York, Texas & Mexican and Gulf Western Texas and Pacific Railway, was chosen Vice President and General Manager of the S.A. and A.P. Railway.[6] Six years later, Monserrate became the pivotal figure in White's extortion scheme.

For a pseudonym, White adopted the strange alias of X Ray. No records show why he chose this unusual sobriquet. Perhaps it was White's way of poking fun with grim humor at his deteriorating condition as he may have been x-rayed either at San Quentin or at some medical institution to confirm the diagnosis of tuberculosis.

After formulating his strategy, White went directly to Fort Worth, Texas where he wrote the following letter (errors included) to General Manager Monserrate:

Ft. Worth, Texas. May 30, 1898
Mr. M.D. Monserrate, General Manager, S.A. & A.P.R.R.
San Antonio:

Dear Sir: We want $7000.00 from your Rail Road, and we will have it let the consequences be what they may to life and property, or there will be no trains running on your Road in four months from now. We have studied this business well and know we can win or we will destroy half the Rail Roads in this country.

After one settlement has been made with us you will never be bothered by us anymore. We are not fooles enough to think you will give this money up until we have convinced you we mean business and have you completely in our power. Pleas do not think for one moment that after we have distroyed a few bridges and wrecked a train or two we will give up in dispair, for we will not. WE GO IN TO WIN.

We will not charge anything for the first two bridges we distroy, but all the work we do after that we charge for each bridge, trestle, or train distroyed $1,000.00, for each human life $2,000.00. As there will be no compromise in this business you will do well to remember the price list, so you will know just how we stand at all times, and whenever you think the account is large enough and you are willing to settle, you can inseart this Advertisement in too of morning papers of San Antonio.

Strayed or Stolen
one red cow, right horn broken off, no brand, $2.50 reward for information. Address X Z this office.

And then you will in a course of a few days received instructions how the money is to paid. We will be in San Antonio in a few days and will let you know when we will begin work so as to give the detectives a fair show.

(Signed) X.Ray & Co.

Not taking any chances, White left Fort Worth after mailing the letter and traveled the hundred plus miles south to Temple, Texas. Scanning the personals in the San Antonio newspapers and not finding the requested ad, he wrote this follow up letter to Monserrate:

Temple, Bell County, Tex., June 2, 1898
M.D. Monserrate, General Manager S.A. & A.P.R.R.

I wrote you a few days ago from Fort Worth saying we would be in San Antonio in a few days and let you know when we would commence work. We don't think it necessary to come to San Antonio just now, so will write you from this town and let you know that we will commence work some time next week. After the first two jobs we will wait three dayes before we do any more work, so as to give you a chance to decide whether we shall go ahead with the work or not, we hope you will have sence enough to see that with the MATCH and DINAMITE we have you completely in our power far more so than the United States has Spain, a blind man can see how the war with Spain will end, we think our WAR is a moor one sided affair than the Spanish war.

We will go a little slow in regard to human life for a few dayes, but when we see you are going to be bull-headed, we will strik where we think we can do the most harm.

If it was possible that you did not get our letter of May 30th Inseart this Advertisement in the too leading Morning newspapers of San Antonio. (Found- A ladies' satchel, containing a thimble and keys. Owner can have same by calling at this office.) $5000.00 will be added to the $7,500.00 if we should hav to be delayed in writing another letter.

We hope everything was made plane in first letter but if you want any-more information put this ad in aforesaid papers. (X.RAY — we would like more information on that matter)

But $5,000.00 will be added for trouble and delay.

(Signed) X.RAY & CO.[7]

Monserrate received the first letter on June 1 but, considering it the work of a crank, paid no attention to it. Upon receipt of the second letter on June 4 he began to think that the threat might be real. Taking precautionary measures, he made copies of the two letters and sent them to the sheriffs of all the counties that the railroad passed through and to the managers of all the other railroads in Texas.

During the interval White continued checking the personals in the San Antonio newspapers. Not finding the requested ad by June 6, he decided to take action to prove his threats were real. On June 7 he made his way south to Burdett, Texas, eight miles south of Lockhart, intending to burn the cotton platform at the Burdett railroad station.

That evening White was forced to keep out of sight for a period of time as a horseman on guard duty nearly rode him down twice. Waiting until the coast was clear, he set fire to the platform and headed one half mile north to the Aransas Pass railroad bridge number 137. He then ignited the fifty-foot bridge and quickly left the area for San Antonio. Both the cotton platform and the bridge were completely destroyed. Superintendent Berry of the Aransas Pass Railroad investigated the damage and reported to Monserrate that both fires were incendiary in origin.

Realizing the seriousness of the situation, Monserrate inserted the requested ad in *The San Antonio Express* on June 11: "X.Ray — We would like more information on that matter." He then contacted J.H. Mott, Jr. of the San Antonio Detective Agency to help investigate the affair.

After reading the ad on June 11, White immediately typed and mailed a redundant third letter:

San Antonio June 11, 1898
M.D. Monserrate, General Manager S.A.&A.P.R.R. Co.

In reply to personal. We will try and make things as plain as possible, and if we fail to present the case so you can surely understand it, we will grant you an interview, we, of course, to name the place and time, and we will do the best we can to make this business as plain to you as it is to us. If you should desire an interview insert this ad in same paper:

X.Ray — We would like to see you at an early date.

You will be perfectly safe, and we will, for there will be no possible chance for a trap. We can give you no assurance of your own safety except our word. That word we pride ourselves on being good as any man's, though scoundrels of the blackest kind the world may call us. When advertising let ad stay in paper four or five days, so we will be certain to see it.

Old pilings that supported the Aransas Pass railroad bridge number 137 at Burdett, Texas which was burned by Ham White on the night of June 7, 1898. Photo taken by Donaly Brice in May, 1986.

In my first letter I made a demand on you for $7,500 and after a reasonable length of time we would commence to destroy your railroad company's property, and would continue to do so until a settlement was made, charging $1,000 for each bridge, trestle, culvert, station platform, water tank, and the wrecking of a train, and $2,000 for each life that may be lost in the wrecks, also $500 for each watchman we may have to kill for interfering with our work or asking too many questions.

That we would not charge anything for the first two jobs — they were to show you we meant business. That free work was done last Tuesday night. We struck you very light that time when we could have struck you hard, but as we have plenty of time, and I had promised you in a former letter we would go a little slow at the start, so as to convince you how completely you are in our power, before too much harm has been done.

In our last letter we stated that an advertisement would cost you $500. We meant where such advertising was for the purpose of delay, or to get clues for the detectives, but when they were in good faith, with an object in bringing about a settlement, nothing would be charged for the trouble and delay. We are to be the judges in the matter. It is useless for you to place watchmen at your bridges, for one man can do no harm, and if you should place too strong a guard it will compel us to blow up your train with dynamite something we do not want to do, but will do it if necessary, let the consequences be what they may.

If one of us should be killed or captured it would be only that much harder for the railroad, and if we should be all captured, which we do not think possible, could the railroads of this country afford to let the case come to trial in the courts? We think not, for imitators would certainly try to do what we failed to do and some of them would succeed. It will take only a little money to do us the balance of our lives, and then this new industry can die with us. Once made public it can never die.

We will change the form of advertisement from what we had in the first letter. When you get ready for settlement insert this ad in paper.

Personal — X.Ray, we would like to have a settlement with you as soon as convenient.

We will wait until Wednesday, June 15, to see if you wish a settlement or an interview. If we do any work after the ad appears in paper we will not charge anything for said work.

X.RAY & CO.

By the way, was that fellow at Burdett, who rode a grey horse, a watchman of yours? He came very near riding over me on two occasions that night.

The frustration and pathos of a dying man who had outlived his time can certainly be felt when reading White's appeal, "It will take only a little money to do us the balance of our lives . . ."

On June 13 Monserrate received the letter. Choosing to stall for as much time as he could to aid the investigation, he placed the ad for an interview rather than for settlement. The *Express* ran the ad for two days, June 15 and 16.

White read the ad on the fifteenth and mailed another tedious reply to Monserrate at 6 PM:

The charred ends of the pilings burned by Ham White on the night of June 7, 1898. Photo taken by Donaly Brice in May, 1986.

San Antonio, Tex., June 15, 1898
M.D. Monserrate, San Antonio, Texas

Sir — In naming the place of our meeting we will try and make the road you are to go as short and plain as possible, so you will have no trouble in understanding and finding the way.

On Saturday evening, June 18, at 8 o'clock, you are to go out on South Presa street driving a double team hitched to an open topped buggy, or if this buggy has a top, the top must be laid well back, so we can see everything in the buggy. Follow street car line that goes down to the Fair grounds; stop at small street car station where the car lines fork, and take off your coat, and go the remainder of the way in your shirt sleeves; after stopping a couple of minutes proceed on the same road until you pass the Fair grounds. a short distance below the Fair grounds you turn squarely to the left, go east a little over one mile through a lane where

119

there is very little travel; when you come to a plain road with telegraph wires you turn back to the left again and come back to town over that road.

Your must stop about two minutes when you first turn to the left; stop again at the crossing on the first little branch or dry wash in the rough lane, and again at the second branch, and again when you come to the Floresville road. Stop about two minutes at each of these places. Stop again for ten minutes on the first small bridge you come to after turning back to town.

If we see everything is O.K. we will stop you somewhere on this road, by calling out "Hello, there!" You must use the same words in answering us, and then obey orders and everything will be all right.

This is to be a meeting on business, and anything you have with you will be safe, but we would rather you would not carry a gun, for that we would be compelled to take.

If we do not meet you, go over the same road again Sunday night. If you decide for this meeting to take place insert this ad in paper.

    X.Ray — we will be there on time.

If you decide not to meet us and wish to communicate with us insert ad in paper to X.Ray. We can read between the lines.

Be sure the ad appears in Sunday morning's paper.

                  X.RAY

Receiving this letter the next day, Monserrate contacted the San Antonio Detective Agency with the information. The agency quickly formulated a plan in which L.W. Peeler, a detective with the agency, would pose as the general manager at the interview. The object was to glean as much information as possible from the extortionists and to note any details about them that would lead to their identity and arrest. After all arrangements were completed the agency informed Monserrate of their proposed course of action and the following ad was inserted in the *Express* on June 18:

X.Ray — Eyesight bad; cannot travel after dark alone. Can furnish trusted agent.

Reading the ad early in the morning, White immediately composed the following reply and mailed it at 10 AM Monserrate received it that afternoon.

Only a Little Money to Do Us The Balance of Our Lives

San Antonio, Texas June 18, 1898

M.D. Monserrate: — We would rather see you than an agent, but as your eyes are bad, and can't see very well at night your trusted agent can come in our place. We hope you will send a man who will have power, if possible, to settle this business.

If you wish, you can come with this agent. You would be company for each other, and would feel more at ease at this interview. I forgot to state in my last letter that after you passed the small street car station, that you should drive your team not faster than a walk.

We hope the directions were plain enough, so there will be no mistakes made and this meeting postponed any longer than tonight. It will not be our fault if the meeting does not take place, for we will stop the buggy somewhere on the road named whether there is only one man or two in it.

X.RAY

Following instructions exactly, the agent was stopped by a command shortly after 8 PM about a mile east of the Fair grounds. White ordered the man to drive off the road and then appeared with a bandana over his face, armed with a revolver.

Quickly beginning the negotiations, the agent asked the extortionist for assurance that the X Ray group would keep their agreement and accept an amount less than the $7,500 previously demanded. White remarked laughingly, "Well, it will cost nearly a thousand to repair the damage we have done, so we'll accept $6,500 — $6,000 in bills and $500 in gold, and to be brought to us Monday night, June 20, '98 at a place nearer the city, a diagram of which with another letter will reach Mr. Monserrate about noon Monday." As soon as the agreement was reached, White bolted from the area and disappeared.

Another agent had been dispatched to the area to keep watch and observe the routes taken by the extortionists. He was able to give a description of White and the horse he rode, but could only pinpoint the direction from which he had arrived.

The agent that had met with White also gave a detailed description of his physical characteristics, but added that there were three of the extortionists at the meeting. He also claimed that his buggy had been tipped over to prevent a quick departure. Later events prove that the only person involved in the scheme was White. Apparently the agent

121

or agents concocted this story to avoid ridicule and chastisement from their superiors at not being able to handle or overpower one lone man.

A report outlining the above events and observations was sent to Monserrate by the agency on June 19. As a postscript to the report, Manager Mott wrote:

> We do not anticipate any great difficulty in capturing the three men tomorrow, Monday night, and will spare no effort to bag anyone connected with the scheme. You cannot be too cautious in communicating with this office.

As promised, White drafted and posted the following letter early on the morning of June 20 which was received by Monserrate at 11 AM After reading the contents he turned the letter over to the detective agency.

San Antonio, Texas June 20th, 1898
Mr. M.D. Monserrate, general manager S.A. & A.P.R.R. Co.

Dear sir — By agreement made with your trusted agent I name the place for our meeting, very easy of access to him, but very dangerous for me, and your road, if you should break faith with me by making an attempt to have me killed or arrested, which I do not believe you will do. Act square with as tonight and we will be friends to you and the road you represent, and we will do every thing in our power to protect your road from harm in the future, and you can rest assured you will never be called on by any of us again for money.

The place of our meeting tomorrow night will be an old vacant house between Main avenue and Soledad street at the corner of Giraud street.

I don't know the number of the house, but the gate on Main avenue is directly in front of 513, across the street.

Your agent must go in at this gate as near half-past eight o'clock as he can, and walk leisurely around the house and I will hail him with the words: "Well, how is it?" he replying, "All right." Then in a moment or two this disagreeable business can be settled.

Respectfully, X.RAY

During his meeting with the agent on the eighteenth White had named Monday night, June 20, as the specified date to deliver the demanded payment. In his letter of June 20th he referred to the date as tomorrow night which was the twenty-first. The confusion over the correct date was White's fault and, as a result, Monserrate followed the instructions detailed in the letter and sent no one to meet with the extortionist on the twentieth. White, however, went to the designated meeting place, waited until 10 PM and then departed. The next day Monserrate received this final letter postmarked 10 AM:

San Antonio, Texas, June 21st, '98

M.D. Monserrate: — I wrote you yesterday morning naming a place for the meeting with your agent, which should have taken place at half past eight o'clock.

I staid at the place until 10 o'clock, and he did not come. I will name the place once more, if he is not on time tonight or within a few minutes of the time named, we will consider things off for the present and we will leave town tomorrow after looking over the newspaper.

The place of our meeting as named in last letter, is a vacant house that fronts two streets, so it is impossible to mistake the place. It is between Main avenue and Soledad street. At 8:35 tonight, will look for agent to enter the Main avenue gate, which is direct across the street from the door of 513, so there can be no mistake made by me hailing the wrong man. Let him have a lighted cigar in his mouth. I will meet him before he goes very far, saying, "Well, how is it?" if everything is O.K. he replying, "It is all right."

X.RAY[8]

After reading the instructions designating the delivery site of the extortion money, Monserrate probably shook his head in wonder at the gullibility and naivete of the blackmailer. From the beginning he had no intention of giving in to blackmail and now that he knew White's plans, he reported them to various law officials in the city as well as the San Antonio Detective Agency. The meeting with the extortionist was to be carried out as scheduled.

There is no clear answer why White devised such a senseless and inane plan to collect the extortion money. Obviously it was another period of his illogical and ludicrous thinking. Nevertheless, White foolishly kept the appointment.

Prior to the prearranged time set to delivery the money law officers had arrived and stationed themselves around the area. Deputy Sheriffs Jim Irwin, Steve Sandoval, and William Green began patrolling Main Avenue while U.S. Marshal Fred Lancaster and U.S. Assistant District Attorney Redford Sharpe stationed themselves on Soledad Street.[9]

Promptly at 8:30 White met the agent at the appointed location and received the valise which supposedly contained six thousand dollars in cash and five hundred dollars in gold. He assured the agent that the railroad would receive no further monetary demands and that he would instruct his confederates to do no more damage to railroad property.

After concluding the negotiations White headed for Main Avenue. Suddenly confronted by Deputy Sheriff Irwin, the startled blackmailer reached for his .38 calibre revolver but the deputy reacted faster. Shoving a forty-five under White's nose, Irwin ordered him to throw up his hands. He meekly complied and was immediately surrounded by the other officers who quickly marched him off to the Bexar County jail.[10]

There Must Be An End Sometime To This Reckless Wayward Life And I Shudder To Think What It Will Be

White's madcap extortion scheme was so ludicrous that from the beginning it was doomed to failure as noted by *The Daily Light* in their analysis of the folly:

> This is considered one of the most gigantic schemes of blackmail that has ever been perpetrated. It hardly appears reasonable that a man of sound sense would attempt anything like it, and can only be the work of anarchists.[1]

Before locking White in the Bexar County jail, the county officers searched him and found a letter with a California address and signed by Henry Miller. He told the officers this was his name. The crowning disappointment for White was when he learned that the valise he received from the agent contained only newspapers and two whiskey flasks filled with water.[2]

In a preliminary hearing held on the morning of June 24 before Justice Cook, White, who was not represented by counsel, waived examination trial on the charge of conspiracy to commit murder and arson by threats to wreck the Aransas Pass Railroad. Justice Cook set White's bonds at $1,000 and ordered him to appear before the grand jury the next day. Unable to post bond, he was returned to jail.[3]

On the twenty-fifth the grand jury indicted him on the charge of conspiring to destroy and injure railroad property. Citing his attempt to wreck a train on May 15, the indictment read, "to unlawfully willingly and maliciously place obstructions to wit burning up a bridge over which tracks were laid, dynamiting the track and road bed upon the track and road bed of a railroad there situated to wit, the track and road bed of the San Antonio and Aransas Pass Railroad Company, whereby the lives of persons would be endangered." Presiding Judge Green ordered him to be bound over for trial during the fall term in Bexar County District Court.[4]

Later the same day a reporter from *The Daily Light* interviewed White in jail. He told the reporter he was forty-four years old and a native of Texas. When questioned about his extortion scheme, he related:

> I merely wrote the letters for a bluff. I was broke and needed money and thought that was a good way to get it. I was only bluffing when I wrote that I would destroy his road if he refused to accept my proposition. I never did intend to wreck the road, even if I wouldn't get any money.

Offering an explanation for his inept plan to collect the blackmail payment, the dejected extortionist stated:

> Of course, now I see what a fool I was. I am just where I ought to be for making an appointment for a meeting place in the heart of the city. Of course, I thought Mr. Monserrate would act square with me for all my dealings with him were in good faith.

White cleared up the mystery about his supposed confederates or his association with a group of anarchists:

> There is only one man in the party and that's me. I was the one that stopped the buggy at Riverside park, and there were no others with me.
>
> I wrote all the letters myself with the same pencil.

As to his present situation and upcoming trial, White lamented:

> I haven't engaged an attorney yet and don't know what I will do. I've got no money and don't know anybody here. I am not able to give bond, and my case will not be tried until next fall, as court adjourns today, I believe.[5]

From late June until late October White languished in the Bexar County jail. On October 21, 1898, in the Thirty-Seventh Judicial District of Bexar County District court, he finally came to trial. When brought before the court and jury he was represented by a court-appointed attorney and pled not guilty to the charge of conspiracy. According to the Bexar County Criminal Minutes:

> After hearing the plea of the defendant and the charge of the Court, delivered the following verdict to wit: "We the Jury find the defendant

105

37th Judicial District.	**The State of Texas,** COUNTY OF BEXAR
No. *1537*	To any Sheriff of the State of Texas—GREETING:
THE STATE OF TEXAS VERSUS *Henry Miller*	YOU ARE HEREBY COMMANDED to take the body of_____ *Henry Miller* _____ if to be found in your County, and him safely keep, so that you may have him when required before the Honorable District Court of the 37th Judicial District, in and for Bexar County, at the Court House thereof, in the City of San Antonio, to answer an indictment exhibited against him wherein he is charged with the offense of *Conspiracy to destroy a union railroad*
CAPIAS.	HEREIN FAIL NOT, under the penalty of the law, but of this Writ and your services thereon make due return on or before the first Monday in *October* _____A. D. 189 *8*
To____ J____ Term. A. D. 180... Filed *June 27* 189 *8* *Nat Lewis* Clerk District Courts Bexar County. By *J W Gibson* Deputy.	WITNESS, NAT. LEWIS, Clerk of the District Court of Bexar County and Seal of said Court, at my office in San Antonio, this *25* day of *June* A. D. 189 *8* *Nat Lewis* Clerk District Courts Bexar County.
Came to hand *June 25* A. D. 189 *8* and executed *June 27* 189 *8* the within named defendant being confined in the Bexar Co Jail *Jno P Campbell* Sheriff *Bexar* County. By *Joseph Van Riper* Deputy. Guessaz & Ferlet, Expert Printers, 161 E. Commerce.	[ISSUED SAME DAY.] By *J W Gibson* Deputy.

guilty as charged in the indictment and assess his punishment at confinement in the penitentiary for a term of two years.

John Dolan, foreman."

When asked if he had anything to say, White tersely answered, "Nothing." The Court passed the following sentence, as quoted from the Criminal Minutes:

The sentence of the Court is that you Henry Miller be taken to the County Jail from where you came and from thence be taken to the State Penitentiary at Huntsville and there be confined at hard labor for the full term of two years in accordance with the judgement herein.[6]

White remained in the Bexar County jail until November 5 when he was transferred to the Texas State Penitentiary. *The Daily Light* gave this report:

Captain A.L. Carmichael, Texas state convict contractor, left for Huntsville yesterday with eighteen prisoners convicted at the October term of the Thirty-Seventh District court on the following charges: . . . . Conspiracy to murder — Henry Miller (X Ray), two years.[7]

Arriving at Huntsville on the fifth, White was registered as Henry Miller, convict no. 17144. Not knowing his actual identity, the prison officials did not consider him a dangerous criminal. It was the first time they had encountered Henry Miller and his sentence to serve two years for conspiracy was not a major criminal offense. Consequently, on the day he arrived the prison officials transferred him to the William Dunovant Prison Farm No. 1 located at Matthews in the south-eastern corner of Colorado County. This was a decision that the prison officials would later regret.

Except for his name, White gave the prison personnel correct information about his background just as he had at other penal institutions. He even made known his prison record at San Quentin.

The Texas State Penitentiary records reveal the following information obtained from him: "Age — 45; Date of Birth — 1853; Height —5'11"; Weight— 150 lbs; Complexion — Light; Eyes — Blue; Hair — Brown; Occupation — Shoe laster; Use of Tobacco — No; Nativity — Texas; Style of Whiskers when received — Mustache; Has no Wife, Parents or Children; Residence — Bastrop, Texas; Habits of Life — Temporate; Education — Fair; Able to Read and Write — yes; Number of Years at School — Four Years; Relations Address — Bastrop, Texas; if Ex-Convict what County sent from — State of Arizona, Year — 1890, Under what Name — Henry Miller, What Force Discharged from — San Quentin, California; Marks, Scars, General Remarks — Bald Head, Two Vaceen Scars on Left Arm, Bad Scar on Left Knee Cap, Right Knee Stiff; Wears No. 7 Shoe."[8]

Apparently conditions were very lax at the prison farm and White bided his time. Out of one hundred and twenty-five prisoners on hand at Prison Farm No. 1 during a two-year period from November, 1898 to November, 1900, there were five escapees, one of whom was Ham White.[9]

For seven months he strictly followed the prison farm rules and regulations while keenly observing all the routines and schedules of the prison personnel. White's escape took place on June 16, 1899 when he apparently walked away from the prison farm and disappeared. The prison officials obviously considered an escape of a convict sentenced for two years on a minor charge of so little consequence that they did not even bother to report it to the newspapers.[10]

Although the authorities in Texas were seemingly unconcerned with White's escape, officers in California certainly were as they were fully aware of his background since 1888 and had found out about his escape from the prison farm. On July 5, 1899 Southern Pacific Railway Company's Chief Special Agent C.C. Crowley in San Francisco issued a wanted circular for Henry Miller alias "X Ray," fearing he had returned to California. The circular cited White as "a desperate stage robber, train robber and wrecker, and a dangerous man to be at liberty."[11]

Although free, White faced the dilemma of having nowhere to go or no one he could turn to for help. He did not dare return to his ex-wife in Erath County where he could be identified as Henry Miller. Freedom no longer held the same value as it had in the past for the broke, forty-five-year-old man suffering from tuberculosis. In desperation White headed for the only refuge left open to him, his brother John's home in the Cedar Creek community near Bastrop. It had been eighteen years since White had made any known contact with his family and he must have been extremely apprehensive as to his reception there.

Any fears of rejection that White might have had were put to rest when he reached his brother's home. The old outlaw might not have been welcomed with open arms but he was still family. In a letter to the author from Mrs. Laura Cunningham, a great-niece of Ham White who has collected much genealogical material on the White family, the following description is given on the reunion of the two brothers:

> This is a family story as told to me by Viola White Gentry, a daughter of John White (Ham's younger brother).

> Her sister Beulah White Davis remembers seeing Ham. She was a young girl (born 1892) and Ham came to the White farm and her father (John) and Ham walked down to the tank (pond, lake, we call it tank). Kid-like, the children ran down to the tank to see what was going on. Her father chased them back to the house. She guessed they wanted to talk in private.[12]

Mrs. Beulah White Davis, at age ninety-five, is still living at this writing. In February, 1987 the author contacted Mrs. Davis in Austin and she kindly consented to be interviewed. As Mrs. Davis is now hard

7.11.

CIRCULAR.

WANTED

Department of Special Agent Southern Pacific Company

SAN FRANCISCO, CAL., July 5, 1899.

To Peace Officers:

The attached photograph is that of **HENRY MILLER,** alias **"X Ray,"** ex-convict No. 14579 of San Quentin, Cal., who recently escaped from the penitentiary of Texas, being now at large. He is wanted by the authorities of Texas.

Miller is a desperate stage robber, train robber and wrecker, and a dangerous man to be at liberty. He may return to California and be now within the State. I therefore desire to call to your attention the above facts and respectfully request that you keep a lookout for him, to the end that he be arrested and returned to the Texas authorities.

HENRY MILLER alias "X RAY"

Description of Henry Miller, alias "X Ray": A laborer; age 46; height 5 feet 9⅞; complexion florid; eyes gray; hair light and thin; bald in front of head; weight about 160; size of foot, 6½; large features, medium ears; nose large at base and pointed; large mouth and thick lips; right leg and ankle stiff; walks lame, caused by chronic rheumatism.

If arrested, wire

C. C. CROWLEY,
Chief Special Agent S. P. Co., Pacific System,
San Francisco.

(7-5-99—1200.)

130

John White, brother of Ham White, and his wife Josie Dyer White. Photograph taken in the 1890s. Furnished to author by Mrs. Laura Cunningham of Austin, Texas, great-niece of Ham and John White.

131

of hearing, the interview was conducted through her daughter, Mrs. Dorothy Cavitt. Remarkably, Mrs. Davis has a vivid recollection of Ham White's visit to her home in June of 1899. Traveling 88 years back in time, here are the remembrances of a seven-year-old child, the only person living today who actually met Ham White.

It was dusk when seven-year-old Beulah White saw her uncle, Ham White, ride up to her parent's home on a light-colored horse. That evening, the excited young girl watched her mother sew material into a type of belt with pouches and widen the hems of her uncle's underwear. Apparently her parents supplied him with what little money they could spare. Being curious, she listened as her uncle told her parents that he never took money from a woman or a child. Overcoming any shyness, she asked her uncle a lot of questions, for which she disappointedly received no answers. She vaguely remembers his persistent cough, not realizing he was suffering from tuberculosis.

Knowing her mysterious uncle had spent the night at her home, she arose at the crack of dawn the next morning. Rushing from the house, she saw her father and uncle walking to the water tank, engaged in serious conversation. Her curiosity aroused, she followed them to the water tank to overhear their conversation, only to be caught and sent back to the house by her father. She did notice that her father and her uncle were very much alike, both being slight built and wiry. Shortly after this her uncle rode off; however, she did find out why he left so suddenly — he was wanted by the law and her parents were afraid to let him stay for fear her older brother Frank White would find out and accidentally talk about it. After Ham White rode off that morning, she never saw him again.[13]

Whether Ham White informed his brother about the circumstances that brought him to the White farm is not known but regardless, he was given refuge. Leaving his brother's farm on the light-colored horse, which was probably stolen, White somehow obtained a firearm and by early July had made his way to Llano County, around eighty miles to the northwest.

Seeing no other way to obtain money, White became a footpad, resorting to the degrading crime of robbing individuals on the road. This must have been quite a downfall and painful experience for a man who had been described as "the most daring, skillful, accomplished highwayman of whom history gives an account." What would have really shattered White, if he had been aware of it, was that this ignoble act would be the last criminal exploit of his career.

On the night of July 6, six miles west of Llano on the Llano and Mason public road, White attempted his first robbery. The holdup ended in utter failure as the victim refused to stop. The old bandit did not give up easily and the next morning his efforts proved more successful.

At the same location at 10 AM he stopped two Fort Worth salesmen named Block and Simon. Encountering no resistance from the two men, he relieved them of $115 and a gold watch. Completing the holdup, White released his victims and disappeared.[14]

White quickly headed away from Llano in a westward direction. To mislead any pursuers, he changed course and by circling through pastures and fields he was able to pass safely through the town of Llano the same night. He then made his way eastward, passing through Click, Round Mountain, and Dripping Springs. After this grueling trek without adequate rest, White reached the eastern edge of Hays County on the night of July 9. Here the exhausted bandit fell into a deep and much needed sleep.[15]

White's two victims wasted no time in reporting the holdup to the Sheriff's office in Llano. Deputy Sheriff Frank H. Hargon and C.S. Stondenmier started at once in pursuit of the robber. For three days and three nights the two determined officers relentlessly trailed White eastward into Hays County. At daybreak on the morning of July 10, the two weary officers found him still asleep and had no trouble capturing the drowsy bandit. Searching his clothing and baggage, the officers found ninety-two dollars remaining of the stolen money.[16]

The fatigued officers headed back to Llano with their prisoner in tow, arriving there on July 11. After being locked up in the Llano County jail, White reverted back to his old Colorado alias of Henry W. Burton. Even though the ruse worked and no one recognized him as Henry Miller, White's facade was finally struck down. After an infamous career of twelve years, the persona of Henry Miller ceased to exist. This, in turn, brought on the resurgence of Ham White.

On the day White was jailed at Llano, many curious people flocked to the jail to get a look at him. One of the visitors was County Assessor Davis who had previously known the bandit. Upon viewing the prisoner Davis immediately identified him as Ham White. As onlookers con-

The remains, as they appear in 1986, of the John White home in the Cedar Creek community of Bastrop County, Texas. This is where Ham White found refuge after his escape from the William Dunovant Prison Farm on June 16, 1899. Photo taken by Donaly Brice in May, 1986.

tinued to visit the jail to see the robber, many of them also identified him as White. Unable to counteract all this confirming evidence, the beaten outlaw finally admitted to being the notorious Ham White. As a result of this capture and identification the citizens of Llano collected a total of sixty dollars and gave it to the highly credited officers, Hargon and Stondenmier.

The newspapers made the most of White's capture and earlier history with the following headlines: "Notorious Ham White, The Old And Daring Stage Robber Believed To Be In Jail" from Austin's *Daily Statesman* and "Noted Stage Robber Identified" from *The Daily Light* in San Antonio.[17]

Because of the attention given to White in the newspapers, his relatives in and around Bastrop learned of his arrest. Some of his family still had feelings for him. Two of them were his nephews, Frank White and Homer Murchison, who visited him in the Llano jail on July 17.[18]

Another nephew, Eugene A. Murchison, after reading the article printed in *The Daily Statesman* on July 13, entered this sad but touching note in his diary:

> Read in morning paper of the capture of Ham White up in the edge of Hayes County. He had robbed some men near Llano and was making his escape when captured. There must be an end sometime to this reckless wayward life and I shudder to think what it will be.[19]

At the time Murchison did not realize how prophetic his writing was or how close the end was coming to White's wayward and reckless life.

White remained in the Llano County jail from July until his trial in mid-December. Knowing his chances for acquittal were slim, especially since his identity had been established, he obtained the services of attorneys Lauderdale and Opp. On December 11 his case came to trial under Judge M.D. Slator in Llano County District Court. Arraigned on the charge of robbery, White pled not guilty and a jury was impaneled with J.W. Fowler selected as foreman. The indictment was then read and all evidence was submitted to the jury. The jury was charged to present a verdict and retired until the next day.

Brought back to court, White dejectedly received the following verdict from the jury:

> We the jury find the defendant guilty as charged in the indictment and assess the penalty fifteen years in the penitentiary.

He was remanded to jail to await official sentencing by the Court.[20]

On December 21 White was scheduled to appear for sentencing but, before it could be passed, his attorneys made two motions — one for a new trial and the other to arrest the judgment found on December 12. Judge Slator refused and overruled both motions. They then filed a motion of an appeal to the Court of Criminal Appeals in Austin and were granted ten days for a statement of facts to be prepared. After a recess, Judge Slator sentenced White to serve fifteen years at the Texas State Penitentiary at Huntsville. He was remanded to jail to await delivery to prison by the sheriff of Llano County.[21]

On January 13, 1900 White left Llano for Huntsville, his sixth term

The State of Texas)
No.2033, Vs.   )   Dec. 12, 1899.
H A M   W H I T E)

    Now on the 11th day of December A.D. 1899, this cause
was called for trial, and the State appeared by her District Attorney,
and the defendant Ham White appeared in person, in open court, his counsel also being present, and the said defendant, Ham White having been duly arraigned, and having pleaded not guilty to the indictment herein,
both parties announced ready for trial, and thereupon a jury, to wit:
J.W.Fowler and eleven others, was duly selected, impaneled and sworn,
who, having heard the indictment read and the defendant's plea of not
guilty thereto, and having heard the evidence submitted, and having been
duly charged by the Court, retired in charge of the proper officer to
consider of their verdict, and afterwards, to wit: on the 12th day of
December A.D.1899, were brought into open court by the proper officer,
the defendant and his counsel being present, and in due form of law returned into open court the following verdict, which was received by the
Court and is here now entered upon the minutes of the court, to wit:
"We the jury find the defendant guilty as charged in the indictment and
assess the penalty fifteen years in the penitentiary, J.W.Fowler, Foreman." It is therefore considered and adjudged by the Court that the
defendant Ham White is guilty of robbery, as found by the jury, and that
he be punished as has been determined by the jury, that is, by confinement in the penitentiary for fifteen years, and that he be remanded to
jail to await the further order of this court herein.

in a penal institution. *The Daily Express* in San Antonio not only reported his delivery to the penitentiary but also his escape from the prison farm and an exaggerated account of his former exploits:

> Austin, Texas. Jan. 14 — Ham White, the notorious stage robber and highwayman, was taken to the State penitentiary at Huntsville today to serve a sentence of fifteen years for holding up and robbing two traveling salesmen near Llano a few months ago. He was convicted in the district court at Llano and brought here last night. Twenty years ago White was one of the most daring stage robbers in the West. He operated in Southwest Texas and is said to have the record of holding up four stages in one day. He worked alone. He eluded capture for several years, but was finally run down by Capt. Lee Hall. He was tried and sentenced to a long term in the penitentiary. He escaped from the convict farm at Eagle Lake about a year ago and at once resumed his old vocation.[22]

The newspaper was in error not only about the time of his escape but also the location of the prison farm. This is understandable as in 1900 there were two William Dunovant Prison Farms in Colorado County. Prison Farm No. 2 was located at Eagle Lake and Prison Farm No. 1, where White made his escape, was at Matthews.[23]

Finally, during his second term in Huntsville, the identities of Henry Miller and Ham White converged. On January 14 he was entered as Ham White and registered as convict no. 19371. The prison officially, now fully aware of his infamous history, kept him at the main prison compound in Huntsville. His prison record states:

> 15 years / Llano. Concurrent with the Llano County term is an unexpired term from Bexar County for conspiracy to destroy and injure railroad.[24]

The following letter from Warden W.W. Waid verifies and confirms without a doubt that Henry Miller and Ham White were the same man. The evidence came to light in November, 1941 when Mrs. Walter Humphery, a great-niece of Ham White, wrote to the Texas State Prison at Huntsville for information regarding her notorious relative.

RE: Ham White, No. 19371, alias Henry Miller, No. 17144

Dear Madam:

In reply to your letter of November 12th, please be advised the above captioned subject was first received in this institution as Henry Miller,

19371

The State of Texas   )
No. 2033, Vs.   )   Dec. 21, 1899.
H A M   W H I T E .   )

This day this cause being again called, the defendant Ham White was brought into open court, in person in charge of the sheriff, for the purpose of having the sentence of the law pronounced in accordance with the verdict and judgment herein rendered and entered against him on a former day of this term. And thereupon the defendant Ham White was asked by the Court whether he had anything to say why said sentence should not be pronounced against him, and he answered nothing in bar thereof. Whereupon the Court proceeded, in the presence of the said defendant Ham White, to pronounce sentence against him as follows: It is the order of the Court that the defendant Ham White, who has been adjudged to be guilty of Robbery, and whose punishment has been assessed by the verdict of the jury at confinement in the penitentiary for fifteen years, be delivered by the sheriff of Llano County, Texas, immediately to the superintendent of the penitentiaries of the State of Texas, or other person legally authorized to receive such convicts, and the said Ham White shall be confined in said penitentiaries for fifteen years in accordance with the provisions of the law governing the penitentiaries of said state. And the said Ham White is remanded to jail until said sheriff can obey the directions of this sentence. And inasmuch as notice of appeal herein has been given, execution of this sentence will be stayed until such time as the Court of Criminal Appeals may affirm this case.
- -

our No. 17144, on November 5th, 1898. He was sentenced from Bexar County October 21st, 1898 for two (2) years under Conspiracy to Destroy and Injure Railroad Property. He escaped June 16, 1899 and was later recaptured.

On January 14th, 1900 he was returned to this institution as Ham White, No. 19371, under sentence of 15 years (which absorbed the unexpired portion of his previous two year term) from Llano County, Texas. He was sentenced on this charge December 14, 1899 for Robbery.

Our records further show he had served a previous term in 1899 in Arizona as Henry Miller. However, we do not have further information but assume that it must have been a Federal conviction since our records state that he was sentenced in the state of Arizona and discharged from San Quentin, California . . .

. . . W.W. Waid, Warden[25]

Aside from two minor errors, the sentencing date from Llano which was actually December 21, 1899 and the year of conviction in Arizona which was in 1891, this letter clearly settles this controversy.

Now back under maximum security and suffering from the advanced stages of tuberculosis, one would assume that White would finally resign himself and accept his fate. But the old outlaw refused to give up. White wanted his freedom but there was no way he could escape so he turned again to the legal system and had his lawyers, Lauderdale and Opp, push for the appeal of his Llano County conviction. Even if his conviction was overruled he still had to serve approximately one year and five months remaining of his Bexar County sentence, but that was better than fifteen years.

White's appeal was presented at the Criminal Court of Appeals in Austin, Texas before Judge W.I. Davidson on April 18, 1900. It was based on the following points: (1) That the prosecution stated that the defendant [White] took one hundred dollars in United States currency from the prosecuting witness (Simon) and that the prosecution failed to show that a portion of the currency was in silver certificates and national bank notes which were not United States currency. (2) Statements made by White to Deputy Sheriff Hargon while in jail could not be used as admissible evidence against him in court.

The court ruled that it is not necessary for the state to prove that all said money was United States currency and that White had been properly warned before making any statement in jail and that such statement could be used as admissible evidence against him. Finding no error in the record, the court upheld White's conviction and sentence rendered by the Llano County District Court and judgment was affirmed.[26]

Fighting for his appeal was the last hurrah for the noted highwayman and having lost it seemed to take the heart out of him. During the months from April through September White's physical condition grew steadily worse. Realizing that he was dying and no longer a threat the prison officials transferred him on September 27, 1900 to the Wynne Farm, a convict sanitarium located on the western edge of Huntsville.[27]

The original Texas State Prison Unit known as "The Walls" located in downtown Huntsville. This unit is still in use. Photograph taken in the 1930s. Courtesy: Texas Department of Corrections, Huntsville, Texas.

CHAPTER TWELVE

Peace To His Ashes

The Wynne Farm was used strictly for convicts suffering from tuberculosis. All convicts confined at the farm were required, if able, to do light garden work. Most of the produce from the farm was used by the prison system and any excess was sold on the open market. The Texas State Penitentiaries Biennial Report for 1902 stated:

> It is gratifying to me [Superintendent Searcy Baker] to be able to report that many convicts received at this farm in a very feeble condition are discharged from it greatly improved, and some entirely cured.[1]

Ham White was not one of them.

He knew he was dying and maybe even welcomed it. Up to this point in his life, White had spent his entire criminal career alone, made no close friends and had no associates in or out of prison. Being a loner throughout his life was one thing, but he did not want to die alone. After his transfer to the Wynne Farm, he turned to the chaplain of the penitentiary, Reverend Samuel H. Morgan, for help. Three years younger than White, Reverend Morgan had been a boyhood friend of the bandit in Bastrop County and had signed his pardon petition in 1881.

In his last days, with Reverend Morgan's help and support, the frightened White repented his wrongdoings and chose to spend his remaining days a Christian. Those remaining days were very short indeed for exactly three months after his transfer, on the morning of December 27, 1900, Hamilton White, III died of tuberculosis.

White was buried in the prison cemetery on the day he died. There were no family members nor friends in attendance, only some of the prison personnel and Reverend Morgan, who stated: "We attended his funeral and saw him properly buried. . . . His race is now run . . . Peace to his ashes."[2]

There were no headline stories or vivid accounts of his life in the newspapers. The only report of his death appeared in *The Bastrop Advertiser*. It was a month later when *The Lockhart Weekly Post* picked up the story in which they gave a brief history of his career and reported in error that he died in the Rusk Penitentiary. They did not even report the date of his death.[3] In this new century, Ham White was a forgotten man.

All this is understandable for by 1900 the days of the highwayman were over. The death of White spelled the death of a legend, the departure of the most noted stage robber in United States history, and, in this author's estimation, the most renowned but unsung outlaw to grace America's frontier. Yes, there were the Jameses, the Youngers, the Daltons, Bill Doolin, and Butch Cassidy and his Wild Bunch, but they all worked as gangs. Every crime, escape, and scheme that White executed, he did entirely on his own. What other outlaw or desperado equalled his record?

Unrecognized for so long, White's memorable career as a knight of the road are relived in this narrative. The intention of this book is not to exalt White but to acknowledge him for the part he played in the history of America's western frontier: in retrospect, perhaps these words printed so long ago in the *Daily Democratic Statesman* are more prophetic, "Let us give the devil his due." Appropriately, as a final note, are Reverend Morgan's farewell words to Ham White in the prison cemetery at Huntsville, Texas, "His race is now run . . . Peace to his ashes."

Entrance to the Joe Byrd Cemetery at Huntsville, Texas where prisoners of the State Penitentiary, including Ham White, are buried. Photo taken by Gayle Metcalf of the Texas Department of Corrections.

Possible grave site of Ham White. Many of these graves have no name or number but this particular grave is located where a prisoner who died in 1900 would be buried. Photo taken by Gayle Metcalf of the Texas Department of Corrections.

Notes

INTRODUCTION

1. (a) Joseph Henry Jackson, *Bad Company*, pp. 119–214. (b) Richard Dillon, *Wells Fargo Detective*, pp. 167–208. (c) Carl W. Breihan, *Lawmen And Robbers*, pp. 1–10.

2. N.A. Jennings, *A Texas Ranger*, p. 298.

3. The following are the only books known by the author that mention White in any detail: (a) Jennings, pp. 294–298; (b) Dora Neill Raymond, *Captain Lee Hall of Texas*, pp. 84–86; (c) Ed Bartholomew, *The Biographical Album of Gunfighters*, no page number, listed alphabetically under the letter W; (d) Eugene B. Block, *Great Stagecoach Robbers of the West*, pp. 234–236.

4. (a) *Andy Adams' Campfire Tales*, Edited by Wilson M. Hudson, pp. xxii–xxiii and 165–169. (b) *The Denver Republican*, July 1, 1881 and *The Denver Tribune*, July 2, 1881. Colorado Historical Society, Denver, Colorado. These newspapers reported the names of the passengers on the robbed stagecoach:

M.M. Engleman	S.B. Nichols
A.E. Walton	Mrs. Baker
A.D. Hadman	John B. Anderson
S.H. Eanil	J.K. Stevens
F.B. Cutler	S.A. Ahpot
O.E. McKee	Mr. Harrison
L.P. McMillien	James Downard — driver

5. (a) *41 Stories By O. Henry*, pp. 266–277. (b) J.S. Gallegly, "Background and Patterns of O. Henry's Texas Badman Stories," *The Rice Institute Pamphlet*, Volume XLII, October, 1955, Number 3, pp. 10–14.

6. RG 28, Post Office Department, Bureau of Chief Inspector, 1877–1879, Box 1, File 1, U.S. vs. Ham White alias H.W. Burton, Robbery of U.S. Mail. National Archives, Washington, D.C.

7. *The Daily Democratic Statesman* (Austin), March 31, 1877. Eugene C. Barker Texas History Center, University of Texas, Austin, Texas.

CHAPTER ONE

1. (a) *The Ancestors and Descendants of Hamilton White and his wife Tabitha Hutchings who came to Bastrop County, Texas in 1836*. Furnished to author by Mrs. Laura G. Cunningham of Austin, Texas, great-niece of Ham White. (b) *Family Recollections — Hamilton White*. Furnished to author by Mrs. Laura G. Cunningham of Austin, Texas, great-niece of Ham White.

2. (a) *The Ancestors and Descendants of Hamilton White and his wife Tabitha Hutchings*. (b) Kenneth Kesselus, *Bastrop County Before Statehood*, pp. 151–178, 181, 216, 242, 250, 296.

3. (a) *The Ancestors and Descendants of Hamilton White and his wife Tabitha Hutchings*. (b) Bastrop County Deed Indexes; listed under the names Hamilton, Ham, H., Tabitha W., and T.W. White. Bastrop County Clerks Office, Bastrop, Texas. (c) 1860 Bastrop County, Texas Census, page 86. Texas State Archives, Austin, Texas. (d) 1860 Bastrop County, Texas Agricultural Census, Schedule 4, Ham White, Number 15. Texas State Archives, Austin, Texas. The Agricultural Census listed the following livestock as belonging to White: 10 horses; 110 cattle; 4 oxen; 30 hogs; valued at $1,600.

4. (a) *The Ancestors and Descendants of Hamilton White and his wife Tabitha Hutchings*. (b) 1850 Bastrop County, Texas Census, page 183; 1860 Bastrop County, Texas Census, page 86. Texas State Archives, Austin, Texas.

5. *The Handbook of Texas*, Walter Prescott Webb, Editor-in-Chief, Volume I, pp. 121–122; Volume II, p. 83.

6. Texas State Penitentiary Convict No. 17144, Henry Miller [alias for Ham White], Texas Department of Corrections Record Book, #15894 through #17813, p. 417. Texas Department of Corrections, Huntsville, Texas.

7. (a) The State of Texas Federal Population Schedules, Seventh Census of the United States, 1860, Volume IV, p. 1873. (b) *Family Recollections — Hamilton White*. (c) RG 204, Application for Clemency, Ham White, Record H, File H–46, Year 1879. National Archives, Washington, D.C.

8. (a) *The Houston Daily Telegraph*, June 21, 1867. Eugene C. Barker Texas History Center, University of Texas, Austin, Texas. (b) Bastrop County Probate Record Book G, p. 74. Bastrop County Clerks Office, Bastrop, Texas. These records state the date of Hamilton White's death was June 14, 1867.

9. Bastrop County Probate Record Book G, pp. 74, 105; Bastrop County Probate Minute Book E, pp. 453, 467, 479. Bastrop County Clerks Office, Bastrop, Texas.

10. RG 204, Application for Clemency, Ham White. Included in these records is an article titled "Stand and Deliver" from *The Wheeling Evening Standard* (West Virginia), June 2, 1877, a four column interview and autobiography of Ham White. This is the only account of White's actions from the day of the Rowe killing until the stage robberies in March, 1877.

11. (a) *The Daily Democratic Statesman* (Austin), March 29, 1877. Eugene C. Barker Texas History Center, University of Texas, Austin, Texas. (b) The State of Texas vs. Ham White, Bastrop County Criminal Indictments; # 1595 for theft of red steer, dated August 6, 1875, # 1640 for theft of steer, # 1641 for theft of cow, # 1642 for theft of cattle, # 1643 for theft of two beef steers, # 1644 for theft of cow, # 1645

for theft of steers, dated December 1, 1875, Bastrop County District Court Criminal Minutes, Volume A, pp. 163, 194. Bastrop County District Clerks Office, Bastrop, Texas. Although the cattle theft occurred in Caldwell County, all indictments were issued from White's home county of Bastrop.

12. *The Daily Democratic Statesman*, March 29, 1877.

13. RG 204, Application for Clemency, Ham White.

14. (a) *The Bastrop Advertiser*, October 9, 1875. Eugene C. Barker Texas History Center, University of Texas, Austin, Texas. (b) *The Daily Democratic Statesman*, October 9, 1875.

15. *The Daily Democratic Statesman*, March 31, 1877.

16. RG 204, Application for Clemency, Ham White.

17. (a) Executive Record Book, Governor Richard Coke, Records of the Secretary of State, Texas, p. 91. Texas State Archives, Austin, Texas. (b) *The Bastrop Advertiser* ran the reward proclamation on October 16, 23, 30, and November 6 and 13, 1875.

18. *The Daily Democratic Statesman*, October 13, 1875.

19. (a) The State of Texas vs. Ham White, Bastrop County Criminal Indictment # 1639 for murder, Bastrop County District Court Criminal Minutes, Volume A, p. 194. (b) The State of Texas vs. Ham White, Bastrop County Criminal Indictment # 1595 for theft of red steer, Bastrop County District Court Criminal Minutes, Volume A, p. 205.

20. RG 204, Application for Clemency, Ham White.

21. Carl Coke Rister, *Fort Griffin on the Texas Frontier*, pp. 161–196.

22. (a) RG 204, Application for Clemency, Ham White. (b) *The Daily Express* (San Antonio), April 24, 1877. Eugene C. Barker Texas History Center, University of Texas, Austin, Texas.

CHAPTER TWO

1. (a) RG 204, Application for Clemency, Ham White, Record H, File H–46, Year 1879. National Archives, Washington, D.C. In the application files, White stated that he took four hundred and six dollars and ten cents. (b) *The Daily Express* (San Antonio), April 24, 1877. Eugene C. Barker Texas History Center, University of Texas, Austin, Texas. The article stated that the amount taken was one hundred sixty dollars from the passengers plus twenty dollars and a quantity of postage stamps taken from the mail. This amount was what the passengers and driver reported, which is probably the correct sum. (c) J.S. Gallegly, "Background and Patterns of O. Henry's Texas Badman Stories," *The Rice Institute Pamphlet*, Volume XLII, October, 1955, No. 3, pp. 10–11. The author claimed that White took one thousand dollars from the Tennessee youth and returned two hundred dollars. All documented evidence, however, reported White took only one hundred dollars, returning twenty dollars.

2. (a) RG 204, Application for Clemency, Ham White. (b) *The Daily Express*, April 24, 1877.

3. (a) *Family Recollections — Hamilton White*. Furnished to author by Mrs. Laura Cunningham of Austin, Texas, great-niece of Ham White. (b) RG *204*, Application for Clemency, Ham White.

4. RG 204, Application for Clemency, Ham White. (b) *The Daily Express*, April

24, 1877. (c) RG 21, Case Number 592, U.S. vs. Ham White, Western District of Texas, Austin Division, FRC 380846. Federal Archives and Record Center, Fort Worth, Texas.

5. (a) RG 204, Application for Clemency, Ham White. (b) *The Daily Express*, March 30 and April 24, 1877. (c) RG 21, Case Number 593, U.S. vs. Ham White.

6. (a) *The Daily Express*, March 30 and April 24, 1877. (b) *The Daily Democratic Statesman* (Austin), March 31, 1877. Eugene C. Barker Texas History Center, University of Texas, Austin, Texas. (c) RG 21, Case number 591, U.S. vs. Ham White and John Vaughn. (d) Gallegly, p. 11. The author names passenger Corbin as the stage driver and includes a story where White returns a watch to a clergyman because they both belong to the same faith. Apparently this story resulted from White's giving back the watch to Corbin although Gallegly also includes this incident in his article. None of the documentation regarding White's 1877 stage robberies mentions the clergyman incident.

7. *The Daily Express*, March 30 and April 24, 1877.

8. For a comprehensive history of the Texas rangers, see Walter Prescott Webb's, *The Texas Rangers*.

9. *The Daily Democratic Statesman*, March 30, 1877.

10. (a) *The Daily Democratic Statesman*, March 30, 1877. (b) *The Daily Express*, April 24, 1877.

11. (a) Dora Neill Raymond, *Captain Lee Hall of Texas*, pp. 84–86. (b) N.A. Jennings, *A Texas Ranger*, pp. 294–298. (c) *The Daily Express*, April 24, 1877. (d) *The Daily Democratic Statesman*, March 30, 1877. Although the article in the *Statesman* does not specify whether the reward was for the killing of Rowe or stagecoach robbery, it was undoubtedly for the stage robbery as White was arrested and tried solely on this charge.

12. (a) RG 21, U.S. vs. Ham White, Minutes of U.S. District Court, Volume C (May 8, 1866–June 6, 1877), Western District of Texas, Austin Division, pp. 615–619, 621, 622. Federal Archives and Record Center, Fort Worth, Texas. (b) *The Daily Democratic Statesman*, April 17, 1877.

13. RG 21, U.S. vs. John Vaughn, Minutes of U.S. District Court, Volume D (June 7, 1877–July 6, 1896), Western District of Texas, Austin Division, p. 26. Federal Archives and Record Center, Fort Worth, Texas.

14. *The Dispatch* (Lampassas), May 3, 1877. Eugene C. Barker Texas History Center, University of Texas, Austin, Texas.

15. (a) *The Daily Express*, April 24, 1877. (b) *The Dispatch*, May 3, 1877. (c) RG 204, Application for Clemency, Ham White.

16. (a) *The Bastrop Advertiser*, August 13, 1881. Eugene C. Barker Texas History Center, University of Texas, Austin, Texas. (b) RG 204, Application for Clemency, Ham White. (c) State of Texas vs. Ham White, Bastrop County Criminal Indictments #1595 and #1640 through #1645, Bastrop County District Court Criminal Court Minutes, Volume A, p. 432. Bastrop County District Clerks Office, Bastrop, Texas.

17. RG 204, Application for Clemency, Ham White.

18. *The Bastrop Advertiser*, April 2, 1881. Both the article from *The Galveston Daily News* and the rebuttal in the *Advertiser* were printed in this issue.

19. *The Bastrop Advertiser*, April 9, 1881.

20. (a) RG 204, Application for Clemency, Ham White. (b) *The Bastrop Advertiser*, April 9, 1881.

21. (a) Jennings, p. 297. (b) Gallegly, p. 12.

22. *The Bastrop Advertiser*, April 9, 1881.

23. (a) RG 204, Application for Clemency, Ham White. (b) *Report Of The Board Of The West Virginia Penitentiary At Moundsville, W. Va. From December 1, 1880 To October 1, 1882*, (W.J. Johnston, Public Printer, Wheeling, W. Va., 1882), p. 24. West Virginia State Archives, Charleston, West Virginia. (c) *The Wheeling Intelligencer*, March 10, 1881. West Virginia State Archives, Charleston, West Virginia.

CHAPTER THREE

1. (a) *The Galveston Daily News*, March 30, April 9, and April 26, 1881. Eugene C. Barker Texas History Center, University of Texas, Austin, Texas. (b) *The Belton Journal*, April 7, 1881. Eugene C. Barker Texas History Center, University of Texas, Austin, Texas. (c) *The Weekly Statesman* (Austin), May 5, 1881. Eugene C. Barker Texas History Center, University of Texas, Austin, Texas. (d) *The Bastrop Advertiser*, April 9, 1881. Eugene C. Barker Texas History Center, University of Texas, Austin, Texas. (e) Bastrop County Commissioners Court Minutes, Volume B, p. 624. Bastrop County Clerks Office, Bastrop, Texas. The minutes show that William E. Jenkins was elected Sheriff on February 15, 1876.

2. *The San Juan Herald*, October 6, 1881. Colorado State Historical Society, Denver, Colorado.

3. (a) *The Galveston Daily News*, May 13, 1881. (b) *The San Juan Herald*, October 6, 1881.

4. RG 28, Post Office Department, Bureau of Chief Inspector 1877–1879, Box 1, File 1, U.S. vs. Ham White alias H.W. Burton, Robbery of U.S. Mail. National Archives, Washington, D.C.

5. (a) *The Galveston Daily News*, June 11, 1881. (b) *The San Juan Herald*, October 6, 1881. The *Tribune* article was reprinted in this issue of the *Herald*.

6. RG 28, Post Office Department, U.S. vs. Ham White alias H.W. Burton. This file included an article from *The Little Rock Gazette* dated June 16, 1881 describing the robbery.

7. (a) Mark Dugan, *Bandit Years: A Gathering of Wolves*, pp. 99–107. The complete history of White's actions in Colorado is also contained in the above book by the author. (b) *The Denver Tribune*, July 2, 1881. Colorado Historical Society, Denver, Colorado.

8. (a) *The Daily News*, July 1, July 7, and July 29, 1881. Colorado Historical Society, Denver, Colorado. (b) RG 28, Post Office Department, U.S. vs. Ham White alias H.W. Burton.

9. (a) *The Denver Republican*, July 1, 1881. Colorado Historical Society, Denver, Colorado. (b) *The Daily News*, July 29, 1881. (c) RG 28, Post Office Department, U.S. vs. Ham White alias H.W. Burton. (d) Eugene B. Block, *Great Stagecoach Robbers of the West*, pp. 234–236. The description of the robbery is accurate but the author reported that five bandits actually committed the hold-up and that the leader was H.W. Burton, not mentioning the name Ham White.

10. *The Denver Republican*, July 1 and July 9, 1881.

11. *The Denver Republican*, July 1, 1881.

12. (a) *The Denver Republican*, June 30 and July 1, 1881. (b) *The Denver Tribune*, July 2, 1881. (c) *The Daily News*, June 30 and July 1, 1881.

CHAPTER FOUR

1. (a) Mark Dugan, *Bandit Years: A Gathering of Wolves*, pp. 99–107. The complete history of White's actions in Colorado is also contained in the above book by the author. (b) RG 28, Post Office Department, Bureau of Chief Inspector, 1877–1879, Box 1, File 1, U.S. vs. Ham White alias H.W. Burton, Robbery of U.S. Mail. National Archives, Washington, D.C.

2. (a) *The Denver Republican*, July 1 and July 9, 1881. Colorado Historical Society, Denver, Colorado. (b) *The Daily News* (Denver), July 16, 1881. Colorado Historical Society, Denver, Colorado.

3. *The Denver Republican*, July 2, 1881.

4. *The Denver Republican*, July 2 and July 9, 1881.

5. For the life of Charley Allison see the author's book, *Bandit Years: A Gathering Of Wolves*, a history of stage robberies of the Barlow-Sanderson Stage Line during the years 1880 and 1881.

6. (a) *The Denver Tribune*, July 2, 1881. Colorado Historical Society, Denver, Colorado. (b) *The Denver Republican*, July 2, 1881.

7. *The Daily News*, July 16, 1881.

8. *The Daily News*, July 21 and July 30, 1881.

9. The Daily News, July 29 and July 30, 1881.

10. *The Daily News*, August 14, 1881. Billy LeRoy, another stage robber, had been lynched by a mob of citizens in Del Norte, Colorado the previous May. For the life of Billy LeRoy see the author's book, *Bandit Years: A Gathering Of Wolves*, a history of stage robberies of the Barlow-Sanderson Stage Line during the years 1880 and 1881.

11. RG 28, Post Office Department, U.S. vs. Ham White alias J.W. Burton. This file contains *The Denver Tribune*'s article titled "King Of The Highwaymen," dated September 25, 1881. In reference to Billy LeRoy, he had been tried and sentenced to ten years the previous March, but escaped and, as previously reported, lynched in Del Norte after a stage robbery in May.

12. (a) RG 21, Case Number 23, U.S. District Court, Pueblo, Colorado, U.S. vs. Henry W. Burton. Federal Archives and Records Center, Denver, Colorado. (b) RG 28, Post Office Department, U.S. vs. Ham White alias H.W. Burton. (c) RG 21, Application of Hamilton White (otherwise known as Henry W. Burton) for a writ of habeas corpus, Habeas Corpus Case Files transferred to the Western District from the Northern District of New York, Records of the U.S. District Court, Western District of New York. Federal Archives and Records Center, Bayonne, New Jersey.

13. *The San Juan Herald*, October 6, 1881. Colorado Historical Society, Denver, Colorado.

14. RG 60, Department of Justice, Source Chronological File (Colorado), Nos. 270 and 271. National Archives, Washington, D.C.

15. (a) RG 60, Department of Justice, Instruction Book L. National Archives, Washington, D.C. (b) RG 28, Post Office Department, U.S. vs. Ham White alias H.W. Burton.

16. (a) RG 28, Post Office Department, U.S. vs. Ham White alias H.W. Burton. (b) *The San Juan Prospector*, December 17, 1881. Colorado State Historical Society, Denver, Colorado. (c) *The San Marcos Free Press*, December 15, 1881. Texas State Archives, Austin, Texas.

17. *The San Marcos Free Press*, December 15, 1881.

18. *The San Marcos Free Press*, July 6, 1882.

19. (a) *The Albany Argus*, June 4, 1882. New York State Library, Albany, New York. (b) General Register of Prisons, House of Corrections, Detroit, Michigan, Volume October 1, 1877–December 26, 1883, p. 227. Burton Historical Collections, Detroit Public Library, Detroit, Michigan. (c) RG 60, Department of Justice, Source Chronological File (East Michigan). National Archives, Washington, D.C.

20. (a) RG 21, Application of Hamilton White (otherwise known as Henry W. Burton) for a writ of habeas corpus. (b) RG 60, Department of Justice, Instruction Book M. National Archives, Washington, D.C. (c) *The Albany Argus*, June 4, 1882. (d) *Albany County Penitentiary Book*, Entry June 3, 1882. Albany Hall of Records, Albany, New York.

CHAPTER FIVE

1. (a) *The Albany Times*, January 20, 1887. New York State Library, Albany, New York. (b) *The Albany Journal*, January 20, 1887. New York State Library, Albany, New York. (c) RG 21, Application of Hamilton White (otherwise known as Henry W. Burton) for writ of habeas corpus, Habeas Corpus Case Files transferred to the Western District from the Northern District of New York, Records of the U.S. District Court, Western District of New York. Federal Archives and Records Center, Bayonne, New Jersey. (d) Mark Dugan, *Bandit Years: A Gathering of Wolves*, pp. 106–107.

2. The State of Texas vs. Ham White, Bastrop County Criminal Indictment # 1639 for murder, Bastrop County District Court Criminal Minutes, Volume B, p. 191. Bastrop County District Clerks Office, Bastrop, Texas.

3. *The Ancestors and Descendants of Hamilton White and his wife Tabitha Hutchings who came to Bastrop County, Texas in 1836.* Furnished to author by Mrs. Laura G. Cunningham of Austin, Texas, great-niece of Ham White.

4. *The Daily Light* (San Antonio), June 26, 1898. San Antonio City Library, San Antonio, Texas.

5. (a) *The San Antonio Daily Express*, July 31, 1887. Eugene C. Barker Texas History Center, University of Texas, Austin, Texas. (b) *The Daily Democratic Statesman* (Austin), July 31, 1887. Eugene C. Barker Texas History Center, University of Texas, Austin, Texas. (c) RG 21, Case No. 1047, U.S. vs. Ham White, Western District of Texas, Austin Division, Criminal Case Files FRC 380848. Federal Archives and Record Center, Fort Worth, Texas.

6. *The Lockhart Register*, August 5, 1887. Eugene Clark Public Library, Lockhart, Texas.

7. RG 21, Case No. 1047, U.S. vs. Ham White.

8. Texas State Penitentiary Convict No. 17144, Henry Miller, Texas Department of Corrections Record Book #15894 through #17813, p. 417 and Texas State Penitentiary Convict No. 19371, Ham White, Texas Department of Corrections Record Book #17814 through #19766, p. 520. Texas Department of Corrections, Huntsville, Texas. The identification of Henry Miller as an alias for Ham White was established by the Texas State Penitentiary at Huntsville, Texas in 1899. A complete explanation of how this transpired is given in the final chapter of this book.

9. Letters: Dr. C. Richard King of Stephenville, Texas to author, dated May 13 and May 18, 1987.

10. (a) Erath County Marriage Book, Volume D, p. 221. Erath County Clerks Office, Stephenville, Texas. (b) *The Los Angeles Times*, March 31, 1891. California State Historical Society, Sacramento, California. (c) *The Arizona Republican* (Phoenix), June 16, 1891. Department of Library, Archives and Public Records, Phoenix, Arizona. (d) *The Handbook of Texas*, Walter Prescott Webb, Editor-in-Chief, Volume I, p. 523.

11. T.R. Farenbach, *Lone Star, A History of Texas and the Texans*, pp. 608–617.

CHAPTER SIX

1. (a) *The San Angelo Standard*, October 1, 1887. *The San Angelo Standard-Times* Office, San Angelo, Texas. (b) *The Waco Examiner*, October 1, 1887. Texas State Archives, Austin, Texas. (c) RG 21, Case No. 216, U.S. vs. J.A. Newsome, Western District of Texas, Waco Divsion. Federal Archives and Records Center, Fort Worth, Texas.

2. (a) *The San Angelo Standard*, October 8, 1887. (b) *The Waco Examiner*, October 5, 1887. (c) Rick Miller, *The Train Robbing Bunch*, pp. 92–93 and 96–99. In this biography of train robber Eugene Bunch, the author gives an accurate account of the stage robberies, the arrest of Newsome and Gray, and the trial of Newsome.

3. RG 21, Case No. 216, U.S. vs. J.A. Newsome.

4. *The Waco Examiner*, October 5, 1887.

5. *The Galveston Daily News*, April 23, 1888. Texas State Archives, Austin, Texas.

6. (a) *The San Angelo Standard*, October 15 and October 22, 1887. (b) *The Waco Examiner*, October 15, October 16, and November 16, 1887. (c) RG 21, Case No. 216, U.S. vs. J.A. Newsome.

7. (a) RG 21, Case No. 216, U.S. vs. J.A. Newsome. (b) *The Waco Examiner*, December 10, 1887. (c) *The San Angelo Standard*, December 17, 1887, January 7 and January 14, 1888.

8. (a) *The San Angelo Standard*, April 21 and April 28, 1888. (b) *The Galveston Daily News*, April 22, April 23, and April 25, 1888.

9. (a) *The Galveston Daily News*, April 25, 1888. (b) William Stanley Hoole, *The Saga of Rube Burrow*, pp. 7, 8, 24–38. Ironically, Rube Burrow was living on a small farm three miles from Stephenville at the same time White lived in Erath County. Although White never associated with the Burrow gang, one wonders if the two men ever met.

10. (a) *The San Angelo Standard*, April 21, 1888. (b) *The Galveston Daily News*, April 22, 1888.

11. *The San Angelo Standard*, April 28, 1888.

12. (a) *The San Angelo Standard*, May 5, 1888. (b) RG 21, U.S. Circuit Court, Northern District, Dallas Division, Minute Book Number 4, p. 118. Federal Archives and Records Center, Fort Worth, Texas.

13. (a) *The Galveston Daily News*, June 25, June 27, and June 29, 1888. (b) *The San Angelo Standard*, June 30, July 14, and October 20, 1888.

(a) *The San Angelo Standard*, October 13, 1888. (b) *The Galveston Daily News*, October 9, 1888.

15. *The San Angelo Standard*, October 20, 1888.

16. (a) *The San Angelo Standard*, September 1, 1888 and June 15, 1889. (b) RG 21, Case No. 216, U.S. vs. J.A. Newsome. (c) RG 21, U.S. Circuit Court, Northern Division, Dallas District, Minute Book Number 4, p. 118. Federal Archives and Records Center, Fort Worth, Texas. (d) *The Waco Daily News*, December 15, 1890. Waco Public Library, Waco, Texas.

17. RG 21, U.S. District Court, Western District of Texas, Waco Division, Criminal Dockets, Vol. 1, Entry 48–W–169. Federal Archives and Records Center, Fort Worth, Texas.

18. (a) *The San Angelo Standard*, December 20, 1890. (b) RG 21, Case No. 216, U.S. vs. J.A. Newsome.

19. *The Waco Daily News*, December 15, 1890.

20. *The Los Angeles Times*, March 31, 1891.

21. *The Ancestors and Descendants of Hamilton White and his wife Tabitha Hutchings who came to Bastrop County, Texas in 1836.* Furnished to author by Mrs. Laura G. Cunningham of Austin, Texas, great-niece of Ham White.

CHAPTER SEVEN

1. RG 28, Records of the U.S. Post Office, Correspondence and Report Relating to Criminal Investigations, Box 77, November, 1888. National Archives, Washington, D.C.

2. *The Arizona Weekly Enterprise* (Florence), December 1, 1888. Department of Library, Archives and Public Records, Phoenix, Arizona.

3. (a) *The Arizona Weekly Enterprise*, November 24 and December 1, 1888. (b) Criminal Case No's. 20, 21, 22, Territory of Arizona vs. Henry Miller, District Court, Pinal County, Arizona, Precinct No. 5, Office of the Clerk of the Superior Court, Pinal County, Florence, Arizona. (c) *The Los Angeles Times*, March 29, 1891. California State Historical Society, Sacramento, California. (d) RG 60, Department of Justice, Justice File #6206-91. National Archives, Washington, D.C. (e) RG 28, Records of the U.S. Post Office, November, 1888.

4. *The Arizona Weekly Enterprise*, November 24, 1888.

5. *The Daily Democratic Statesman* (Austin), March 30, 1877. Eugene C. Barker Texas History Center, University of Texas, Austin, Texas.

6. (a) *The Arizona Weekly Enterprise*, December 1, 1888. (b) Criminal Case No's. 20, 21, 22, Territory of Arizona vs. Henry Miller.

7. *The Arizona Weekly Enterprise*, December 1, 1888.
8. Criminal Case No's. 20, 21, 22, Territory of Arizona vs. Henry Miller.
9. *The Arizona Weekly Enterprise*, December 15, 1888.
10. (a) *The Arizona Weekly Enterprise*, December 15, 1888. (b) *Register and Descriptive List of Convicts in the Territorial Prison, Arizona*, Convict No. 556, Henry Miller. Department of Library, Archives and Public Records, Phoenix, Arizona. (c) *Discharge Book, Territorial Prison, Yuma, Arizona*, Convict No. 556, Henry Miller, Department of Library, Archives and Public Records, Phoenix, Arizona.
11. RG 2, Records of the U.S. Post Office, November, 1888.
12. (a) RG 28, Records of the U.S. Post Office, November, 1888. Letter from D.O. Herbert to Acting Chief Post Office Inspector James Maynard dated May 16, 1891. (b) RG 28, Records of the U.S. Post Office, Correspondence and Reports Relating to Criminal Investigations, Box 117, April, 1891. National Archives, Washington, D.C.
13. RG 60, Department of Justice, Justice File #6206-91. Letter from Henry Miller to the United States Attorney General, dated June 8, 1891.
14. RG 28, Records of the U.S. Post Office, November, 1888.
15. (a) RG 60, Department of Justice, Justice File #6206-91. (b) *The Arizona Sentinal* (Yuma), June 6, 1891. Department of Library, Archives and Public Records, Phoenix, Arizona.
16. RG 60, Department of Justice, Justice File #6206-91.
17. *1891-1892 Biennial Report to the Governor by M.M. McInernay, Superintendent*. Department of Libray Archives and Public Records, Phoenix, Arizona. (b) *The Arizona Silver Belt*, January 4, 1896. Department of Library, Archives and Public Records, Phoenix, Arizona.
18. (a) RG 60, Department of Justice, Justice File #6206-91. (b) *Register and Descriptive List of Convicts in the Territorial Prison, Arizona*, Convict No. 556, Henry Miller. (c) William H. Haught, *The Arizona Territorial Prison* (looseleaf binder form, typescript). Department of Library, Archives and Public Records, Phoenix, Arizona.
19. *The Los Angeles Times*, March 29 and March 31, 1891. California Historical Society, Sacramento, California.
20. *The Los Angeles Times*, April 1, 1891.
21. *The Los Angeles Times*, March 31, 1891.
22. (a) RG 28, Records of the U.S. Post Office, Correspondence and Reports Relating to Criminal Investigation, Box 77, November, 1888. National Archives, Washington, D.C. (b) RG 28, Records of the U.S. Post Office, Correspondence and Reports Relating to Criminal Investigations, Box 117, April, 1891. National Archives, Washington, D.C. This file contains two articles from *The San Francisco Chronicle and Examiner*: "A Lone Stage Robber near Redding" dated March 8, 1891 and "A Stage Held Up" datelined March 7, 1891. (c) *The Los Angeles Times*, April 1, 1891.
23. RG 28, Records of the U.S. Post Office, April, 1891. *The Los Angeles Times*, April 1, 1891.
24. *The Los Angeles Times*, April 1, 1891.
25. (a) RG 28, Records of the U.S. Post Office, April, 1891. (b) *The Los Angeles Times*, March 29, 1891.

26. *The Los Angeles Times,* March 29 and April 1, 1891.
27. *The Los Angeles Times,* March 29, 1891.
28. *The Los Angeles Times,* April 1, 1891.
29. *The Los Angeles Times,* March 29, 1891.

CHAPTER EIGHT

1. *The Los Angeles Times,* March 29 and March 31, 1891. California Historical Society, Sacramento, California. (b) *The Los Angeles Herald,* March 30, 1891. Bancroft Library, University of California, Berkeley, California. (c) RG 28, Records of the U.S. Post Office, Correspondence and Reports Relating to Criminal Investigations, Box 77, November, 1888 and Box 117 April, 1891. National Archives, Washington, D.C.
2. *The Los Angeles Times,* March 31, 1891.
3. *The Los Angeles Times,* March 29, 1891.
4. *The Los Angeles Herald,* March 30, 1891.
5. *The Los Angeles Times,* March 31, 1891.
6. (a) *The Los Angeles Times,* March 31 and April 1, 1891. (b) RG 28, Records of the U.S. Post Office, November, 1888 and April, 1891.
7. RG 60, Department of Justice, Justice File #6206-91. National Archives, Washington, D.C. This file contains an article titled "A Card" from *The Arizona Weekly Enterprise* (Florence), dated June 6, 1891.
8. *The Los Angeles Times,* April 1, 1891.
9. *The Los Angeles Times,* April 1, 1891.
10. (a) RG 28, Records of the U.S. Post Office, November, 1888 and April, 1891. (b) Criminal Case Numbers 20, 21, 22, Territory of Arizona vs. Henry Miller, District Court of Pinal County, Arizona, Precinct No. 5. Office of the Clerk of the Superior Court, Pinal County, Florence, Arizona.
11. (a) *The Los Angeles Times,* March 29, and March 31, 1891. (b) RG 28, Records of the U.S. Post Office, November, 188 and April, 1891.
12. *The Los Angeles Times,* April 5, 1891.

CHAPTER NINE

1. RG 60, Department of Justice, Justice Files #6206-91. National Archives, Washington, D.C. This file contains an article from *The Arizona Weekly Enterprise* (Florence), dated June 6, 1891.
2. RG 21, Records of the District Court of the U.S. for the Territory of Arizona, Second Judicial District, 1878–1912 Criminal Cases, Box 5, Case Numbers 206, 207, 230; Minute Records, 1877–1912, Box 3, pp. 17–18. Federal Archives and Records Center, Laguna Niguel, California.
3. RG 21, Records of the District Court of the U.S. for the Territory of Arizona, Second Judicial District, 1878–1912 Criminal Cases, Box 5, Case Numbers 206 and 207, Demurrer; Minute Records, 1877–1912, pp. 22–23. Federal Archives and Records Center, Laguna Niguel, California.

4. RG 21 Records of the District Court of the U.S. for the Territory of Arizona, Second Judicial District, Minute Records, 1877–1912, pp. 46, 47, 48, 62, 85, 91, 92; Criminal Records, 1885–1911, Register of Criminal Actions and Fee Book, Box 1, p. 30. Federal Archives and Records Center, Laguna Niguel, California.

5. RG 60, Department of Justice, Justice Files 6206-91. This file contains an article from *The Arizona Enterprise* dated June 6, 1891.

6. RG 60, Department of Justice, Justice Files 6206-91. Letter: Henry Miller to United States Attorney General, Washington, D.C.

7. (a) *The Arizona Sentinel* (Yuma), June 13, 1891; (b) *The Arizona Republican* (Phoenix), June 16, 1891; (c) *The Arizona Daily Star* (Tucson), June 19, 1891. Department of Library, Archives and Public Records, Phoenix, Arizona.

8. (a) *The Arizona Republican*, June 16, 1891. (b) *The Arizona Daily Star*, June 19, 1891.

9. (a) San Quentin Prison Register, Inmate No. 14579, Henry Miller, F3653-9 (VB 113). California State Archives, Sacramento, California. (b) San Quentin Inmate Identification Card, Reg. No. 14579, Henry Miller. California State Archives, Sacramento, California.

10. RG 60, Department of Justice, Justice Files 6206-91. Letter: Henry Miller to United States Attorney General, Washington, D.C., October 28, 1891.

11. RG 60, Department of Justice, Justice Files 6206-91. Letter: Henry Miller to United States Attorney General, Washington, D.C., November 26, 1891.

12. RG 60, Department of Justice, Attorney General Instructions, Vol. 17, p. 475. National Archives, Washington, D.C.

13. RG 60, Department of Justice, Justice Files 6206-91. Letter: U.S. Attorney Thomas F. Wilson, Tucson, Arizona to United States Attorney General, Washington, D.C., December 23, 1891.

14. (a) San Quentin Prison Register, Inmate No. 14579, Henry Miller. (b) San Quentin Inmate Identification Card, Reg. No. 14579, Henry Miller. (c) James B. Hume and Jno. N. Thacker, *Wells, Fargo & Co's. Robbers Record*, p. 91. Included in the text is the complete merit system and credits allowed year by year, used by the California State Prison.

CHAPTER TEN

1. Texas State Penitentiary Convict No. 19371, Ham White, Texas Department of Correction Record Book #17814 through #19766, p. 520. Texas Department of Corrections, Huntsville, Texas.

2. *The Ancestors and Descendants of Hamilton White and his wife Tabitha Hutchings who came to Bastrop County, Texas in 1836* and *Family Recollections —Hamilton White*. Furnished to author by Mrs. Laura G. Cunningham of Austin, Texas, great-niece of Ham White.

3. *The Daily Light* (San Antonio), June 26, 1898. San Antonio City Library, San Antonio, Texas.

4. (a) T.R. Fehrenbach, *Lone Star A History of Texas and the Texans*, pp. 613–631. (b) *The Handbook of Texas*, Walter Prescott Webb, Editor-in-Chief, Volume I, pp. 585, 716–717, 822–823; Volume II, pp. 393, 429–430.

5. (a) *The San Antonio Daily Express*, May 17, 1898. Eugene C. Barker Texas History Center, University of Texas, Austin, Texas. (b) District Court of Bexar County, Case No. 15371, The State of Texas vs. Henry Miller, Conspiracy. Bexar County Clerks Office, San Antonio, Texas.

6. S.G. Reed, *A History of the Texas Railroads*, pp. 242–249. (b) *The Handbook of Texas*, Walter Prescott Webb, Editor-in-Chief, Volume II, pp. 542.

7. *The Daily Light*, June 22, 1898. These two letters written by White as X Ray, dated May 30, 1898 and June 2, 1898, were printed in this issue of *The Daily Light* with all grammatical errors intact. They are reproduced in this book as originally written.

8. *The Daily Light*, June 24, 1898. The remainder of the letters written by White as X Ray were printed in this issue of *The Daily Light* with all grammatical errors corrected. They are reproduced in this book as such.

9. *The Daily Light*, June 22, 1898.

10. *The Daily Light*, June 22 and June 24, 1898.

CHAPTER ELEVEN

1. *The Daily Light* (San Antonio), June 24, 1898. San Antonio City Library, San Antonio, Texas.

2. *The Daily Light*, June 22, 1898.

3. *The Daily Light*, June 24, 1898.

4. (a) District Court of Bexar County, Case No. 15371, The State of Texas vs. Henry Miller, Conspiracy. Bexar County Clerks Office, San Antonio, Texas. (b) *The Daily Light*, June 26, 1898.

5. *The Daily Light*, June 26, 1898.

6. (a) District Court of Bexar County, Case No. 15371, The State of Texas vs. Henry Miller, Conspiracy. (b) Criminal Minutes, District Court, Bexar County, Texas, October Term, 1898, pp. S46, S47. Bexar County Clerks Office, San Antonio, Texas. (c) *The Daily Light*, October 22, 1898.

7. *The Daily Light*, November 6, 1898.

8. (a) Texas State Penitentiary Convict No. 17144, Henry Miller, Texas Department of Corrections Record Book #15894 through #17813, p. 417. Texas Department of Corrections, Huntsville, Texas. (b) Texas State Penitentiary, Description Of Convict When Received, Register No. 17144, Henry Miller. Texas Department of Corrections, Huntsville, Texas.

9. *Biennial Report Of The Superintendant Of Texas State Penitentiaries For Two Years Ending October 31, 1900*, p. 29. Texas State Archives, Austin, Texas.

10. Texas State Penitentiary Convict No. 17144, Henry Miller.

11. Wanted Circular for Henry Miller (Ham White) alias "X Ray," Department of Special Agent Southern Pacific Company, San Francisco, California, dated July 5, 1899. Copy furnished to author by Mr. Fred White, Jr., Bryan, Texas, who owns the original circular.

12. Letter: Mrs. Laura Cunningham, Austin, Texas, great-niece of Ham White, to author, dated April 14, 1886.

13. Taped interviews with Mrs. Beulah White Davis, niece of Ham White,

through her daughter, Mrs. Dorothy Cavitt, in Austin, Texas, February 14 and April 17, 1987. Author's collection.

14. *The San Antonio Daily Express*, July 8, 1899. Eugene C. Barker Texas History Center, University of Texas, Austin, Texas.

15. *The Daily Statesman* (Austin), July 13, 1899. Eugene C. Barker Texas History Center, University of Texas, Austin, Texas.

16. (a) *The San Antonio Daily Express*, July 11 and July 12, 1899. (b) *The Daily Statesman*, July 13, 1899.

17. (a) *The Daily Light*, July 12, 1899. (b) *The Daily Statesman*, July 13, 1899.

18. *Diary of Eugene A. Murchison*, entry dated July 17, 1899. Furnished to author by Mrs. Laura G. Cunningham of Austin, Texas, great-niece of Ham White.

19. *Diary of Eugene A. Murchison*, entry dated July 13, 1899.

20. (a) The State of Texas vs. Ham White, Case No. 2033, Minutes, Llano County District Court, November Term, 1899. Vol. F, p. 333. Llano County Clerks Office, Llano, Texas. (b) *The Daily Statesman*, December 13, 1899.

21. The State of Texas vs. Ham White, Case No. 2033, Minutes, Llano County District Court, November Term, 1899, Vol. F, pp. 357, 358.

22. *The San Antonio Daily Express*, January 15, 1900.

23. *Biennial Report Of The Superintendent Of State Penitentiaries For Two Years Ending October 31, 1900*, p. 29. Texas State Archives, Austin, Texas.

24. Texas State Penitentiary Convict No. 19371, Ham White, Texas Department of Corrections Record Book #17814 through #19766, p. 520. Texas Department of Corrections, Huntsville, Texas.

25. Letter: W.W. Waid, Warden of the Texas State Penitentiary at Huntsville to Mrs. Walter P. Humphrey, Temple, Texas, dated November 15, 1941. Furnished to author by Mrs. Laura G. Cunningham of Austin, Texas, great-niece of Ham White.

26. *Texas Decisions Reported In The Southwestern Reporter, Vols. 56, 57, And 58, April, 1900 To December, 1900*, pp. 100–101.

27. Texas State Penitentiary Convict No. 19371, Ham White, Texas Department of Corrections Record Book #17814 through #19766.

CHAPTER TWELVE

1. *Biennial Report Of The Superintendent Of Texas State Penitentiaries For Twenty-Two Months Ending August 31, 1902*, p. 22. Texas State Archives, Austin, Texas.

2. (a) *The Bastrop Advertiser*, January 5, 1901. Eugene C. Barker Texas History Center, University of Texas, Austin, Texas. (b) Texas Penitentiary Convict No. 19371, Ham White, Texas Department of Corrections Record Book #17814 through #19766. Texas Department of Corrections, Huntsville, Texas.

3. (a) *The Bastrop Advertiser*, January 5, 1901. (b) *The Lockhart Weekly Post*, January 31, 1901. Eugene Clark Public Library, Lockhart, Texas.

Bibliography

BOOKS

Andy Adams' Campfire Tales, edited by Wilson M. Hudson (University of Nebraska Press, Lincoln and London, 1976).

Ed Bartholomew, *The Biographical Album of Gunfighters* (The Frontier Press of Texas, Houston, 1958).

Eugene B. Block, *Great Stagecoach Robbers of the West* (Doubleday and Company, Garden City, New York, 1962).

Carl W. Breihan, *Lawmen And Robbers* (The Caxton Printers, Ltd., Caldwell, Idaho, 1986).

Richard Dillon, *Wells, Fargo Detective* (Coward-McCann, Inc., New York, 1969).

Mark Dugan, *Bandit Years: A Gathering of Wolves* (Sunstone Press, Santa Fe, New Mexico, 1987).

T.R. Farenbach, *Lone Star, A History of Texas and the Texans* (American Legacy Press, New York 1983).

41 Stories by O. Henry (A Signet Classic, New American Library, New York and Scarborough, Ontario, 1984).

The Handbook of Texas, Volumes I and II (The Texas Historical Association, Austin, 1952.

William Stanley Hoole, *The Saga of Rube Burrow, King of American Train Robbers And His Band Of Outlaws* (Confederate Publishing Company, University, Alabama, 1981).

James B. Hume and Jno. N. Thacker, *Wells, Fargo & Co's. Robbers Record* (H.S. Crocker & Co., San Francisco, California, 1884).

Joseph Henry Jackson, *Bad Company* (Harcourt, Brace and Company, New York, 1949).

N.A. Jennings, *A Texas Ranger* (Charles Scribner's Sons, 1899).

Kenneth Kesselus, *Bastrop County Before Statehood* (Jenkins Publishing Company, Austin, Texas, 1986).

Rick Miller, *The Train Robbing Bunch* (Creative Publishing Company, College Station, Texas, 1983).

Dora Neill Raymond, *Captain Lee Hall of Texas* (University of Oklahoma Press, Norman, Oklahoma, 1940).

S.G. Reed, *A History of the Texas Railroads* (The St. Clair Publishing Co., Houston, Texas).

Carl Coke Rister, *Fort Griffin on the Texas Frontier* (University of Oklahoma, Norman, Oklahoma, 1956).

Virginia McConnell Simmons, *The San Luis Valley* (Pruett Publishing Company, Boulder, Colorado, 1985).

Texas Decisions Reported In The Southwestern Reporter, Vols. 56, 57, and 58, April 1900 to December, 1900 (West Publishing Co., St. Paul, 1911).

Walter Prescott Webb, *The Texas Rangers* (University of Texas Press, Austin, Texas, 1965).

NEWSPAPERS

The Albany Argus, 1882. New York State Library, Albany, New York.

The Albany Journal, 1887. New York State Library, Albany, New York.

The Albany Times, 1887. New York State Library, Albany, New York.

The Arizona Daily Star (Tucson), 1891. Department of Library, Archives, and Public Records, Phoenix, Arizona.

The Arizona Republican (Phoenix), 1891. Department of Library, Archives, and Public Records, Phoenix, Arizona.

The Arizona Sentinal, (Yuma), 1891. Department of Library, Archives, and Public Records, Phoenix, Arizona.

The Arizona Silver Belt, 1896. Department of Library, Archives, and Public Records, Phoenix, Arizona.

The Arizona Weekly Enterprise (Florence), 1888. Department of Library, Archives, and Public Records, Phoenix, Arizona.

The Belton Journal, 1881. Eugene C. Barker Texas History Center, University of Texas, Austin, Texas.

The Bastrop Advertiser, 1881, 1901. Eugene C. Barker Texas History Center, University of Texas, Austin, Texas.

The Daily Democratic Statesman (Austin), 1875, 1877, 1899. Eugene C. Barker Texas History Center, University of Texas, Austin, Texas.

The Daily Light (San Antonio), 1898. San Antonio City Library, San Antonio, Texas.

The Daily News, 1881. Colorado Historical Society, Denver, Colorado.

The Denver Republican, 1881. Colorado Historical Society, Denver, Colorado.

The Denver Tribune, 1881. Colorado Historical Society, Denver, Colorado.

The Dispatch (Lampassas), 1877. Eugene C. Barker Texas History Center, University of Texas, Austin, Texas.

The Galveston Daily News, 1881, 1887, 1888. Eugene C. Barker Texas History Center, University of Texas, Austin, Texas.

The Houston Daily Telegraph, 1867. Eugene C. Barker Texas History Center, University of Texas, Austin, Texas.

The Lockhart Register, 1887. Eugene Clark Public Library, Lockhart, Texas.

The Lockhart Weekly Post, 1901. Eugene Clark Public Library, Lockhart, Texas.

The Los Angeles Herald, 1891. Bancroft Library, University of California, Berkeley, California.

The Los Angeles Times, 1891. California State Historical Society, Sacramento, California.

The San Angelo Standard, 1887, 1888, 1889, 1890. *The San Angelo Standard-Times* Office, San Angelo, Texas.

The San Antonio Daily Express, 1877, 1898, 1899. Eugene C. Barker Texas History Center, University of Texas, Austin, Texas.

The San Juan Herald, 1881. Colorado Historical Society, Denver, Colorado.

The San Marcos Free Press, 1881, 1882. Texas State Archives, Austin, Texas.

The Waco Daily News, 1890. Waco Public Library, Waco, Texas.

The Waco Examiner, 1887. Texas State Archives, Austin, Texas.

The Wheeling Intelligencer, 1881. West Virginia State Archives, Charleston, West Virginia.

PUBLIC RECORDS

1850 Bastrop County, Texas Census.

1860 Bastrop County, Texas Census.

The State of Texas Federal Population Schedules, Seventh Census of the United States, 1860, Volume IV.

1860 Bastrop County, Texas Agricultural Census.

Bastrop County Commissioners Court Minutes, Volume B. Bastrop County Clerks Office, Bastrop, Texas.

Bastrop County District Court Criminal Minutes, Volumes A and B. Bastrop County District Clerks Office, Bastrop, Texas.

Bastrop County Probate Record Book G and Bastrop County Probate Minute Book E. Bastrop County Clerks Office, Bastrop, Texas.

RG 21, Case Numbers 591, 592, 593, FRC 380846; 1047, FRC 380848, U.S. vs. Ham White, Western District of Texas, Austin Division. Federal Archives and Record Center, Fort Worth, Texas.

RG 21, Minutes of U.S. District Court, Volume C (May 8, 1866–June 6, 1877) and Volume D (June 7, 1877–July 6, 1896), Western District of

Texas, Austin Division. Federal Archives and Record Center, Fort Worth, Texas.

RG 21, Case Number 23, U.S. District Court, Pueblo, Colorado, U.S. vs. Henry W. Burton. Federal Archives and Record Center, Denver, Colorado.

RG 21, Application of Hamilton White (otherwise known as Henry W. Burton) for a writ of habeas corpus, Habeas Corpus Case Files transferred to the Western District of New York from the Northern District of New York, Records of the U.S. District Court, Western District of New York. Federal Archives and Record Center, Bayonne, New Jersey.

RG 21, Records of the District Court of the U.S. for the Territory of Arizona, Second Judicial District, 1878–1912 Criminal Cases, Box 5, Case Numbers 206, 207, 230; Minute Records, 1877–1912, Box 3; Criminal Records, 1885–1911. Federal Archives and Records Centers, Laguna Niguel, California.

RG 21, Case No. 216, U.S. vs. J.A. Newsome, Western District of Texas, Waco Division. Federal Archives and Records Center, Fort Worth, Texas.

RG 21, U.S. Circuit Court, Northern Division, Dallas District, Minute Book Number 4. Federal Archives and Records Center, Fort Worth, Texas.

RG 21, U.S. District Court, Western District of Texas, Waco Division, Criminal Dockets, Vol. 1, Entry 48-W-169. Federal Archives and Records Center, Fort Worth, Texas.

RG 28, Post Office Department, Bureau of Chief Inspector, 1877–1879, Box 1, File 1, U.S. vs. Ham White alias H.W. Burton, Robbery of U.S. Mail. National Archives, Washington, D.C.

RG 28, Records of U.S. Post Office Correspondence and Reports Relating to Criminal Investigations: Box 77, November, 1888 and Box 117, April, 1891. National Archives, Washington, D.C.

RG 60, Department of Justice, Source Chronological File (Colorado), Nos. 270 and 271. National Archives, Washington, D.C.

RG 60, Department of Justice, Source Chronological File (East Michigan). National Archives, Washington, D.C.

RG 60, Department of Justice, Instruction Books L and M. National Archives, Washington, D.C.

RG 60, Department of Justice, Justice File #6206-91. National Archives, Washington, D.C.

RG 60, Department of Justice, Attorney General Instructions, Vol. 17, National Archives, Washington, D.C.

RG 204, Application for Clemency, Ham White, Record H, Year 1879. National Archives, Washington, D.C.

Criminal Case Nos. 20, 21, 22, Territory of Arizona vs. Henry Miller, District Court, Pinal County, Arizona, Precinct No. 5. Office of the Clerk of the Superior Court, Pinal County, Florence, Arizona.

District Court of Bexar County, Case No. 15371, The State of Texas vs. Henry Miller, Conspiracy. Bexar County Clerks Office, San Antonio, Texas.

Criminal Minutes District Court, Bexar County, Texas, October Term, 1898. Bexar County Clerks Office, San Antonio, Texas.

The State of Texas vs. Ham White, Case No. 2033, Minutes, Llano County District Court, November Term, 1899, Vol. F. Llano County Clerks Office, Llano, Texas.

Texas Department of Corrections Record Books, #15894–17813 and #17814–19766. Texas Department of Corrections, Huntsville, Texas.

General Register of Prisons, House of Corrections, Detroit, Michigan, Volume October 1, 1877 through December 26, 1883. Burton Historical Collections, Detroit Public Library, Detroit, Michigan.

Albany County Penitentiary Book, Albany Hall of Records, Albany, New York.

Register and Descriptive List of Convicts in the Territorial Prison, Arizona. Department of Library, Archives and Public Records, Phoenix, Arizona.

Discharge Book, Territorial Prison, Arizona. Department of Library, Archives and Public Records, Phoenix, Arizona.

San Quentin Prison Register, F 3653-9, (VB 113). California State Archives, Sacramento, California.

The Board Of The West Virginia Penitentiary At Moundsville, W. Va. From December 1, 1880 To October 1, 1882 (W.J. Johnston, Public Printer, Wheeling, W. Va., 1882). West Virginia State Archives, Charleston, West Virginia.

1891–1892 Biennial Report to the Governor By M.M. McInernay, Superintendent. Department of Library, Archives and Public Records, Phoenix, Arizona.

Biennial Report Of The Superintendent Of Texas State Penitentiaries for Two Years Ending October 31, 1900 (Von Boeckmann, Moore & Schutze, State Printers, Austin, 1900). Texas State Archives, Austin, Texas.

Biennial Report Of The Superintendent Of Texas State Penitentiaries For Twenty-Two Months Ending August 31, 1902 (Von Boeckmann, Schutze & Co., State Printers, Austin, 1902). Texas State Archives, Austin, Texas.

Wanted Circular for Henry Miller (Ham White) alias "X Ray," Department of Special Agent Southern Pacific Company, San Francisco, California, dated July 5, 1899. Copy furnished to author by Mr. Fred White, Jr., Bryan, Texas, who owns the original circular.

Executive Record Book, Governor Richard Coke, Records of the Secretary of State, Texas. Texas State Archives, Austin, Texas.

Erath County Marriage Book, Volume D. Erath County Clerks Office, Stephenville, Texas.

Bibliography

PERIODICALS

J.S. Gallegly, "Background and Patterns of O. Henry's Texas Badman Stories," *The Rice Institute Pamphlet*, Volume XLII, October, 1955, Number 3.

UNPUBLISHED MANUSCRIPTS

The Ancestors and Descendants of Hamilton White and his wife Tabitha Hutchings who came to Bastrop County, Texas in 1836. Furnished to author by Mrs. Laura G. Cunningham of Austin, Texas.

Family Recollections — Hamilton White. Furnished to author by Mrs. Laura G. Cunningham of Austin, Texas.

Diary of Eugene A. Murchison. Furnished to author by Mrs. Laura G. Cunningham of Austin, Texas.

William H. Haught, *The Arizona Prison.* Department of Library, Archives and Public Records, Phoenix, Arizona.

LETTERS

W.W. Waid, Warden of the Texas State Penitentiary at Huntsville, Texas to Mrs. Walter P. Humphrey of Temple, Texas, dated November 15, 1941. Furnished to author by Mrs. Laura G. Cunningham of Austin, Texas.

Mrs. Laura Cunningham, Austin, Texas, great-niece of Ham White, to author, dated April 14, 1986.

Dr. C. Richard King of Stephenville, Texas to author, dated May 13 and May 18, 1987.

INTERVIEWS

Taped interviews with Mrs. Beulah White Davis, niece of Ham White, through her daughter, Mrs. Dorothy Cavitt, in Austin, Texas, February 14 and April 17, 1987.

Chronology of the Life of Ham White

JANUARY, 1836 — Hamilton White II and wife Tabitha, parents of Ham White, imigrate from Pittsylvania County, Virginia to Bastrop County, Texas.

APRIL 17, 1854 — Ham White born near Bastrop, Texas.

JUNE 12, 1867 — Father of Ham White murdered by James Rowe in Bastrop County.

AUGUST 6, 1875 — White steals a herd of cattle in Caldwell County, Texas.

LATE SEPTEMBER, 1875 — Captured in Milam County, Texas.

EARLY OCTOBER, 1875 — Escapes en route to Caldwell County jail.

OCTOBER 7, 1875 — Murders James Rowe and is wounded and crippled for life by Rowe's brother.

OCTOBER 12, 1875 — Governor of Texas offers a two hundred dollar reward for arrest of Ham White for Rowe's murder.

DECEMBER 1, 1875 — Indicted for the Rowe murder in Bastrop County.

1876 — Hunts buffalo in West Texas.

MID DECEMBER, 1876 — Eludes arrest by the Texas Rangers in West Texas.

LATE WINTER, 1877 — Captured by so-called friends in Brown County, Texas but escapes.

MARCH 7, 1877 — Commits first stagecoach robbery between Waco and Gatesville, Texas.

MARCH 19, 1877 — Stops stage between Georgetown and Salado, Texas.

MARCH 23, 1877 — Robs stage outside Bastrop, Texas.

MARCH 23, 1877 — Robs two stages in one day; in the morning stops the stage from Austin to Lockhart and in the afternoon robs the stage from Austin to San Antonio and takes over one thousand dollars.

MARCH 28, 1877 — Captured by Texas Rangers in Lulling, Texas and incarcerated in Austin jail.

APRIL 13–19, 1877 — Tried and convicted for robbing U.S. mails in U.S. District Court, Austin, sentenced to life imprisonment.

APRIL 23, 1877 — Has photo taken at Marks photographic gallery in Austin.

MAY 1, 1877 — Delivered to West Virginia Penitentiary at Moundsville.

JULY 1, 1879 — Begins quest for pardon.

MARCH 1, 1881 — Pardoned by President Hayes, released on March 8 and returns to Bastrop, Texas.

APRIL 2, 1881 — Arrested by Bastrop County Sheriff for Rowe murder.

APRIL 8, 1881 — Released from jail on bond and leaves area later in month.

MAY 1, 1881 — Attempts but fails to rob stage near Gonzales, Texas.

MAY 11, 1881 — Robs stage near Lampasas, Texas.

MAY 26, 1881 — Holds up stage near Purmela, Texas.

JUNE 1, 1881 — Robs stage near Gainesville, Texas.

JUNE 15, 1881 — Stops and robs two stages at the same time between Fayetteville and Alma, Arkansas, then heads for Colorado.

JUNE 29, 1881 — Commits classic stage robbery near Alamosa, Colorado and arrested, as Henry W. Burton, by City Marshal in Pueblo.

JULY 1, 1881 — While en route to Arapahoe County jail in Denver, jumps train in escape attempt but recaptured.

JULY 28, 1881 — Identified as Ham White.

SEPTEMBER 21–23, 1881 — Tried as Henry W. Burton in U.S. District Court at Pueblo and sentenced to life imprisonment.

SEPTEMBER 24, 1881 — Attempts but fails to escape jail at Pueblo.

OCTOBER 11, 1881 — Considered dangerous, White is ordered by U.S. Attorney General to be imprisoned at Detroit House of Corrections.

DECEMBER 3, 1881 — While en route to Detroit, White attempts to escape and savagely attacks U.S. marshal but is foiled by a woman passenger and is delivered to penitentiary that night.

MAY 24, 1882 — Because of dangerous behavior, White is transferred to Penitentiary at Philadephia, Pennsylvania by U.S. Attorney General.

JUNE 2, 1882 — Penitentiary at Philadephia refuses to take White and he is taken to Albany County Penitentiary at Albany, New York.

JUNE 3, 1882 — Arrives in Albany by train and greeted by huge crowd who want to see the famous stage robber. Delivered to penitentiary.

JANUARY 20, 1887 — Discharged from penitentiary by U.S. District Court Judge because of procedure errors during 1881 trial.

WINTER-SPRING-SUMMER, 1887 — works in shoe factories in Lynn, Massachusetts and returns to Texas.

JULY 28, 1887 — Holds up two stagecoaches between Austin and Fredricks-burg, Texas and flees to Stephenville, Erath County, Texas.

SEPTEMBER 29, 1887 — Holds up two stages on San Angelo-Ballinger stage line, ten miles from Ballinger, Texas.

OCTOBER 3, 1887 — Robs San Angelo-Ballinger stage at same location.

OCTOBER 4, 1887 — Stops Ballinger bound mail buggy at same location.

OCTOBER 9, 1887 — Cowboy James Newsome arrested for the San Angelo-Ballinger stage robberies; convicted and sentenced to life imprisonment in December. He was finally exonerated and freed in December, 1890.

DECEMBER 7, 1887 — Marries Nannie C. Scott in Stephensville.

APRIL 20, 1888 — Robs two more San Angelo-Ballinger stages in same loca-tion as first robberies.

JUNE 23, 1888 — Holds up San Angelo-Ballinger stage near Willow Water Hole Station.

NOVEMBER 23, 1888 — Travels to Arizona and robs travelers and stage from Florence to Casa Grande and foolishly follows stage to Casa Grande where he is arrested next day.

DECEMBER 12–13, 1888 — Tried and convicted in Pinal County District Court as Henry Miller for robbery of Wells Fargo express box and sentenced to twelve years in Arizona Territorial Prison at Yuma.

DECEMBER 15, 1888 — Entered penitentiary and is allowed to work overtime for himself making elegant walking canes and sets up marketing system which distributed his work throughout U.S. Makes enough money by 1891 to send money to his wife in Texas and hire best law firm in southwest to secure pardon.

JANUARY 20, 1891 — Pardoned by acting Governor of Territory of Arizona N. Oakes Murphy and heads for Los Angeles, California where he takes job in cane shop producing walking canes.

MARCH 7, 1891 — Attempts to rob stage near Redding, California but is foiled by shotgun messenger and in gunfight wounds stage driver. Flees to San Francisco.

MARCH 19, 1891 — Returns to Redding and robs stage of fifty dollars worth of gold nuggets.

MARCH 22, 1891 — Returns to Los Angeles and is arrested the next day by U.S. Marshal on U.S. charge of robbing the mail in the 1888 Arizona stage robbery. Suspected by Wells Fargo and U.S. Marshal of robbing Redding stage.

APRIL 4, 1891 — Returned to Florence, Arizona for trial.

MAY 19–20, 1891 — Tried and convicted in U.S. District Court at Florence, Arizona for robbery of U.S. mails.

MAY 26, 1891 — Sentenced as Henry Miller to ten years hard labor in the California State Prison at San Quentin.

JUNE 10, 1891 — While en route to prison, escapes from three sleeping officers in Casa Grande, Arizona and steals watch and money from one of the officers.

JUNE 12, 1891 — After nearly dying of thirst in desert White is captured by three ranchers who turned him over to a U.S. Marshal in Florence.

JUNE 15, 1891 — Imprisoned at San Quentin as Henry Miller.

DECEMBER 23, 1891 — Denied request for transfer to Arizona Territorial Prison at Yuma.

DECEMBER 26, 1897 — Released from San Quentin with merit time. White has contracted tuberculosis while in prison.

DECEMBER, 1897 to May, 1898 — In Nashville, Tennessee.

MAY 15, 1898 — Unsuccessfully attempts to derail and rob train near Kenedy, Texas.

MAY 30, 1898 — Failing to rob train, White devises plan to blackmail San Antonio and Arkansas Pass Railway and sends first of several extortion letters to general manager using alias of X-Ray.

JUNE 7, 1898 — Not receiving answer to extortion letters White burns cotton platform and railroad bridge near Burdett, Texas.

JUNE 18, 1898 — Meets with agent for railway in San Antonio to discuss extortion payment.

JUNE 21, 1898 — During scheduled meeting in San Antonio to collect extortion money White is arrested by local police.

OCTOBER 21, 1898 — Tried and convicted as Henry Miller in Bexar County District Court on charge of conspiring to destroy railroad property and sentenced to two years in State Penitentiary at Huntsville, Texas.

NOVEMBER 5, 1898 — Enters penitentiary as Henry Miller and is transferred to William Dunovant Prison Farm No. 1 at Matthews, Texas.

JUNE 16, 1899 — Escapes from prison farm and finds refuge at home of his brother, John White, near Bastrop, Texas. He had not contacted his family in eighteen years.

JULY 6, 1899 — Attempts but fails to rob travelers on road near Llano, Texas.

JULY 7, 1899 — Robs two salesmen of $115 on road near Llano and flees to Hays County, Texas.

JULY 10, 1899 — Captured by Llano County officers in Hays County.

JULY 11, 1899 — White in Llano jail he is identified by several visitors as Ham White.

DECEMBER 11–12, 1899 — Tried and convicted as Ham White in Llano County District Court for the robbery of the salesmen.

DECEMBER 21, 1899 — Sentenced to fifteen years imprisonment at State Penitentiary at Huntsville, Texas.

JANUARY 14, 1900 — Enters Huntsville as Ham White and unexpired term from Bexar County is added to sentence.

APRIL 18, 1900 — Criminal Court of Appeals in Austin upholds White's Llano County conviction.

SEPTEMBER 27, 1900 — Suffering from advanced stages of tuberculosis, White is transferred to Wynn Farm, a convict sanitarium in Huntsville.

DECEMBER 27, 1900 — Ham White dies at Wynn Farm and is buried in the prison cemetery at Huntsville.

INDEX

Adams, Andy, xvi
Alamosa, Colorado, 40–42, 44, 45
Albade (Lytton Springs), Texas: 60
Albany County Penitentiary, 55, 56, 68, 74
Albany, New York, 55, 56
Alexander, Mr., 7
Alice, Texas, 113
Allen (Texas ranger), 20
Allen, J.J., 12
Allison, Charley (stage robber), 46, 47
Alma, Arkansas, 39, 40
Alpine, Colorado, 40
Andrews and Lessing (attorneys), 72
Arapahoe County jail, 46, 47, 49
Arizona Territorial Prison, 81, 84, 104
Austin, Stephen F., 6
Austin, Texas, 4, 19, 20, 22, 24, 38, 59, 61, 66, 139

Baker and Campbell (attorneys), 84, 95
Baker, Mrs., 43
Baker, Searcy (Superintendent, Texas State Penitentiary), 142
Ballinger and San Angelo Stage Line, 65
Ballinger, Texas, 65, 66, 69, 91
Barlow-Sanderson Stage Line, xiii, 40
Barnes, W.H. (Pinal County District Court Judge), 80
Bartell, J.W., 85, 89, 90
Bastrop, Texas, 4–9, 12, 16, 18, 37, 129, 135
Baughman, Theodore, xvi
Beebee, O.P., 59, 60

Benbrook, Texas, 70
Bennett, Harry, 72
Bentley, H.S. (attorney), 24
Berry (Superintendent, S.A. & A.P. Railroad), 116
Billy the Kid (Henry McCarty alias William Bonney), xv, 47
Black Bart (Charles E. Boles), xv, 92
Blain, M.W. (U.S. Deputy Marshal), 44
Blair's Hollow, Texas, 38
Blanco River (Texas), 19
Blanco, Texas, 60
Block (salesman), 133
Boles, Charles E. (see Black Bart)
Brackett, Ed, 87
Brazee (U.S. Commissioner), 46
Brazos River (Texas), 73
Brewster, Benjamin Harris (U.S. Attorney General), 55
Brice, Donaly, xiii
Bridges, W.L., 26, 32
Brimley, Stephen, 16
Brooks, John A. (Texas ranger), 67
Broom, Armon, 65, 70
Browder, James, 19
Brown, Henry (Alias of Ham White), 78, 80
Brown, John, 72
Brown, W.R., 38
Brownwood, Texas, 16
Bull, J.H. (U.S. Marshal), 72
Bunch, Eugene (train robber), 67
Burdett, Texas, 116
Burrow, Rube (train robber), 70

173

A Note about the Author

Mark Dugan was raised in Jackson County, Missouri and has been studying and researching Western American History since he was a child. As a young adult he lived in Europe, mainly Germany for ten years before returning to the United States. He worked for the U.S. Government much of that time. He is a graduate of North Carolina State University and teaches at Appalachian State University at Boone, North Carolina.

He has written three books on bandits in and of the American West.